take one tomato...

christine france

take one tomato...

and create an unforgettable taste sensation

christine france

southwater

This edition is published by Southwater

Southwater is an imprint of Anness Publishing Ltd
Hermes House, 88–89 Blackfriars Road, London SE1 8HA
tel. 020 7401 2077; fax 020 7633 9499; www.southwaterbooks.com; info@anness.com

© Anness Publishing Ltd 2002

Published in the USA by Southwater, Anness Publishing Inc., 27 West 20th Street, New York, NY 10011;
fax 212 807 6813

This edition distributed in the UK by The Manning Partnership Ltd, 6 The Old Dairy, Melcombe Road, Bath BA2 3LR;
tel. 01225 478 444; fax 01225 478 440; sales@manning-partnership.co.uk

This edition distributed in the USA by National Book Network, 4720 Boston Way, Lanham, MD 20706;
tel. 301 459 3366; fax 301 459 1705; www.nbnbooks.com

This edition distributed in Canada by General Publishing, 895 Don Mills Road, 400–402 Park Centre, Toronto, Ontario M3C 1W3;
tel. 416 445 3333; fax 416 445 5991; www.genpub.com

This edition distributed in Australia by Pan Macmillan Australia, Level 18, St Martins Tower, 31 Market St, Sydney, NSW 2000
tel. 1300 135 113; fax 1300 135 103

This edition distributed in New Zealand by The Five Mile Press (NZ) Ltd, PO Box 33–1071 Takapuna, Unit 11/101–111 Diana Drive, Glenfield, Auckland 10;
tel. (09) 444 4144; fax (09) 444 4518; fivemilenz@clear.net.nz

A CIP catalogue record for this book is available from the British Library.

Publisher: Joanna Lorenz
Managing Editors: Helen Sudell and Linda Fraser
Editor: Jennifer Schofield
Production Controller: Claire Rae
Additional Text: Jenni Fleetwood
Designer: Nigel Partridge
Jacket Design: Balley Design Associates

Previously published as part of a larger compendium, *Tomato*

1 3 5 7 9 10 8 6 4 2

NOTES
Bracketed terms are intended for American readers.

For all recipes, quantities are given in both metric and imperial measures and, where appropriate,
measures are also given in standard cups and spoons.
Follow one set, but not a mixture, because they are not interchangeable.

Standard spoon and cup measures are level.
1 tsp = 5ml, 1 tbsp = 15ml, 1 cup = 250ml/8fl oz

Australian standard tablespoons are 20ml. Australian readers should use 3 tsp in place of 1 tbsp
for measuring small quantities of gelatine, flour, salt, etc.

Medium (US large) eggs are used unless otherwise stated.

CONTENTS

INTRODUCTION

Technically fruit but treated like vegetables, tomatoes combine the best of both. Many varieties are so sweet and succulent that they can be eaten in the hand, like grapes or strawberries. In a savoury setting they are equally at home, making excellent sandwiches, soups and appetizers, as well as contributing to numerous pasta, meat and fish dishes.

When tomatoes were first introduced into Europe, they were greeted with some suspiciòn. Their colour – which was yellow, not red – led to their being called "golden apples". In Germany they were known as "goldapfel", in Italy as "pomo d'oro", and as "pommes d'or" by the French.

Below: Tomatoes can easily be grown in sheltered, sunny gardens.

EARLY CULTIVATION

Tomatoes were first cultivated in England by John Gerard, superintendent of the College of Physicians' gardens in London. Gerard was not particularly impressed by the plant, famously describing it as being "of ranke and stinking savour" and recommending it be grown only for ornamental or medicinal purposes.

The Spanish and Italians were the first Europeans to recognize the potential of tomatoes in cooking, featuring them in recipes from the late 17th century. The early development of new and hardy strains was centred largely around the Mediterranean, and by the middle of the 18th century there were more than 1,000 varieties of tomato cultivated in Spain, Portugal, Italy and the south of France.

Above: Round or salad tomatoes are just one of 7,000 cultivars of tomatoes.

It was soon discovered that tomatoes flourished when cultivated under glass. This extended the growing season and made it easier to grow them in more northerly climes.

It is not certain who was responsible for introducing the tomato to North America, but from the middle of the 18th century, tomatoes were cultivated in Carolina and within the next 50 years they were being grown in Florida.

There are now well over 7,000 varieties of tomatoes worldwide and new hybrids are constantly being introduced, often to meet the needs of massive supermarket chains that wish to have "own brand" tomatoes on their shelves.

NUTRITION

In recent years, tomatoes have caught the attention of health-conscious cooks because of their lycopene content. This natural bioflavonoid is a powerful antioxidant that is believed to lower the risk of cancer, particularly prostate and colon cancer, and heart disease. Not only are tomatoes a good source of vitamins A and C, but they also yield potassium, calcium and other mineral salts. Typically they contain only a trace of fat and just 14 calories/58 kilojoules per 100g/3½oz serving.

PROCESSED TOMATOES

Canned tomatoes are incredibly convenient, and if this means that they are sometimes used rather too freely, so that their flavour dominates rather than complements other ingredients, that is a small price to pay for a high quality, nutritious product that saves time and effort. Canned tomatoes are particularly good in sauces for pastas and pizzas, and can be puréed when passata is called for. The best type for canning are plum tomatoes, which are available whole or chopped.

Passata is another useful pantry item. This product consists of raw, ripe tomatoes that have been puréed and sieved, and can be smooth or chunky. Passata is handy for making soups and sauces. Sieved tomatoes mixed with tomato purée (paste) are marketed as sugocasa. This is more concentrated than passata and is ideal for pizzas and pasta sauces. Look out, too, for creamed tomatoes, which are very smooth and thick.

Sun-dried tomatoes have an intense flavour and are sweet and succulent, especially when they are preserved in olive oil. The oil in which they are packed takes on their flavour and can be used for cooking or to make a fabulous salad dressing.

Tomato purée or paste is a concentrated product with a strong flavour and bright red colour. Small amounts give an intense flavour to stews, sauces and soups. The sun-dried version is even more concentrated than the regular purée or paste. It should be used sparingly and it is often necessary to reduce the quantity of oil in the recipe.

Above: Tomatoes and fresh herbs are a perfect match.

Right: Sun-dried tomatoes preserved in oil can be chopped and added to any dish, or eaten as they are.

COMPANION COOKING

One reason why tomatoes are so consistently popular the world over is the ease with which they combine with other ingredients.

They have a special affinity for the allium family, especially onions and garlic, aubergine (eggplant) and all the peppers, including chillies. They also taste delicious with potatoes, fennel, squashes and green beans.

Although the sweetest varieties do not need much seasoning, tomatoes taste especially good with a variety of herbs and spices. Basil, oregano and marjoram are often cited as perfect companions for tomatoes, but other types of herbs work well too. Try strewing young sage leaves over tomatoes before baking, or toss a little thyme, rosemary or winter savory into a tomato-based stew or casserole. Coriander (cilantro), a herb whose delicate green leaves have a strong, earthy flavour, is good in salads and stews, especially when the latter contain chillies. It is best to add coriander at the last minute, or the subtlety of its flavour will be lost.

Warm spices also go well with tomatoes. In the Middle East, for instance, cinnamon is often used in dishes like the Iranian chicken khoresh, which teams tomatoes with chicken, aubergines and peppers. In goulash, it is paprika that provides the hint of heat, while cumin is the favoured spice in Greek lamb sausages served with a rich tomato sauce.

Tomatoes taste great with all types of meat, especially beef steak and bacon, and they are just as good with poultry, game and fish. Sauces based on canned tomatoes suit the more robust types of fish, like swordfish or fresh tuna, whereas concassed fresh tomatoes would be the better choice for sole or plaice.

Ragu, a wonderful Italian tomato sauce, owes its flavour to fresh plum tomatoes. Although it is perfect for pasta, it is delicious in other dishes too. Try it over polenta, with steak or sausages, in a vegetarian bean bake or as a topping for a baked potato with a dusting of grated Parmesan cheese.

Tomatoes are endlessly versatile and their universal appeal has made them a firm favourite in most kitchens. Whether you like round and sweet cherry tomatoes or deep red beefsteaks, no meal should be without them.

BUYING AND STORING TOMATOES

The best place to buy tomatoes is direct from the grower, from a market gardener's stall or a farmer's market. This is not to suggest that you can't buy good tomatoes at your local supermarket. You can, especially if they stock top quality organic produce, or have developed their own range of tomatoes.

Visit a farmer's market and the experience will be altogether different. The tomatoes will have been allowed to ripen naturally and will not have been transported over vast distances. Those that have been grown organically will have been cultivated using sustainable farming practices, without the use of artificial fertilizers and pesticides. They will have a naturally lower water content and will usually have a better flavour than non-organic alternatives.

Wherever you buy your tomatoes, ripeness and freshness are key words. Vine tomatoes – sold still attached to the stalk or vine – are now a familiar sight in supermarkets as well as market stalls. They smell like home-grown tomatoes, but as the aroma emanates from the stalk and leaves rather than the fruit itself, there is no guarantee that they will taste as good as those grown at home.

Tomatoes come in a variety of shapes and sizes, from tiny cocktail fruit, not much bigger than grapes, to giant beefsteaks weighing up to 1.3kg/3lb. They can be round, plum- or pear-shaped; squat, smooth or ribbed. Although most tomatoes are red, their colours can vary quite considerably – the spectrum runs from pale ivory through to deep purple. Some tomatoes are green even when ripe, and there are also striped varieties. Certain varieties of tomatoes are perfect for snacks and salads, others are best cooked, but all are worth getting to know.

Above: The low water content of plum tomatoes makes them ideal for using in your favourite recipes.

Left: Cherry tomatoes make perfect snacks and are delicious eaten raw or cooked.

Cherry tomatoes are small and dainty. They are high in sugar and low in acid. Easy to eat whole, they make delectable snacks. Serve them raw, either as they are, or filled with delicious pâté. Toss them into salads or chargrill them until they caramelize.

Plum tomatoes are shaped like the fruits for which they are named. They have a low water content and their flesh is meaty, with a substantial core and thick skin. They also have fewer seeds than round tomatoes and their concentrated flavour and high acidity make them ideal in cooked dishes.

Above: Round tomatoes are ideal for cooking.

Right: Giant Beefsteak tomatoes are perfect in salads.

Choosing and Storing Tomatoes
- When selecting tomatoes, choose those with fresh-looking leafy green tops
- Take a sniff: fresh, ripe tomatoes will have the characteristic aroma, not just from the stalks but from the fruit itself
- Depth of colour is a good indication of ripeness
- Ripe tomatoes should be firm, but should yield slightly when lightly pressed
- Tomatoes are best stored at room temperature
- An unripe tomato will redden on a sunny window sill or in a fruit bowl with a ripe banana; however, the flavour won't be as good as when they are allowed to ripen on the plant

Left: Dainty pear tomatoes are the most favoured variety of tomato for garnishing savoury dishes.

Pear tomatoes tend to be quite small. They are wonderful for garnishing savoury platters as they look pretty when fanned. Pear tomatoes are also favoured for their superior taste.

Round or salad tomatoes are the tomatoes we see most often at the supermarket. The flavour varies according to the variety and whether they are grown and picked during their natural season. Look for fruit that are soft and very red. Adding a pinch of sugar will bring out the sweetness and seasoning well with salt and pepper accentuates their flavour.

Beefsteak tomatoes are large, round and squat. They are usually deep red or orange in colour and they have a good proportion of flesh to skin. Due to their low acidity, they are sweet and mellow, making them the ideal tomato for eating raw in salads or sliced as a sandwich filler.

BASIC PREPARATION

Peeling

Add a professional finish to sauces and soups that are not being sieved by peeling and seeding the tomatoes.

1 Use a small, sharp knife to cut out the green stalk then make a cross in the skin on the base of each tomato.

2 Place the tomatoes in a heatproof bowl and pour over boiling water to cover. Leave for 30 seconds, then drain.

3 Once cooled, gently pull away the loosened skin from each tomato.

Concassing

This term is used when tomato flesh is diced for use in sauces or soups.

Peel and seed the tomatoes, then cut the flesh into neat 5mm/¼in squares.

Flame-skinning

This is the simplest way to skin fewer than five or six tomatoes. For more than this, use the boiling water method.

1 Skewer one tomato at a time on a metal fork or skewer and hold in a gas flame for 1–2 minutes, turning the tomato until the skin splits and wrinkles.

2 Remove the tomato from the skewer and leave it to cool on a board.

3 When cool enough to handle, pull off and discard the skins.

Wedging

Wedged pieces of tomato are particularly attractive in fresh salads.

For wedges, cut the tomato in half downwards, then quarter.

Slicing

The appearance of tomato slices depends on whether they are cut vertically or horizontally.

Slice them across for salads and pizzas as they will have a more attractive finish and the seeds will also stay in the flesh.

Seeding

There are two methods that can be used to seed fresh tomatoes.

1 Remove the stalks from the tomatoes and slice the fruit into quarters as above. Carefully slide the blade of a sharp knife along the inner flesh of the tomato, scooping out the pulp and all the seeds.

2 Halve the tomatoes and scoop out the core and seeds with a teaspoon.

The best soups are packed with flavour, and there's nothing better than a few ripe tomatoes to add that extra richness that makes a chilled soup such as Chilled Tomato and Sweet Pepper Soup so special, or a warming Onion and Tomato Soup so comforting. And what better way to start a meal than with the tangy flavour of juicy tomatoes? Try the delectable Griddled Tomatoes on Soda Bread or rustic Baked Polenta with Tomatoes; the possibilities are endless.

Soups and Snacks

CHILLED TOMATO <u>AND</u> SWEET PEPPER SOUP

A RECIPE INSPIRED BY THE SPANISH GAZPACHO, WHERE RAW INGREDIENTS ARE COMBINED TO MAKE A CHILLED SOUP. IN THIS RECIPE THE INGREDIENTS ARE COOKED FIRST AND THEN CHILLED.

SERVES FOUR

INGREDIENTS
  2 red (bell) peppers, halved
  45ml/3 tbsp olive oil
  1 onion, finely chopped
  2 garlic cloves, crushed
  675g/1½lb ripe well-flavoured
    tomatoes
  150ml/¼ pint/⅔ cup red wine
  600ml/1 pint/2½ cups vegetable stock
  salt and ground black pepper
  chopped fresh chives, to garnish
For the croûtons
  2 slices day-old white bread,
    crusts removed
  60ml/4 tbsp olive oil

COOK'S TIP
Any juice that accumulates in the pan after grilling (broiling) the peppers, or in the bowl, should be stirred into the soup. It will add a delectable flavour.

1 Cut each pepper half into quarters and seed. Place skin-side up on a grill (broiling) rack and cook until the skins have charred. Transfer to a bowl and cover with a plate.

2 Heat the oil in a large pan. Add the onion and garlic, and cook until soft. Meanwhile, remove the skin from the peppers and roughly chop them. Cut the tomatoes into chunks.

3 Add the peppers and tomatoes to the pan, then cover and cook gently for 10 minutes. Add the wine and cook for a further 5 minutes, then add the stock and salt and pepper, and simmer for 20 minutes.

4 To make the croûtons, cut the bread into cubes. Heat the oil in a small frying pan, add the bread and fry until golden. Drain on paper towels, cool, then store in an airtight box.

5 Process the soup in a blender or food processor until smooth. Pour into a clean glass or ceramic bowl and leave to cool thoroughly before chilling for at least 3 hours. When the soup is cold, season to taste.

6 Serve the soup in bowls, topped with the croûtons and garnished with chopped chives.

GAZPACHO <u>WITH</u> AVOCADO SALSA

TOMATOES, CUCUMBER AND PEPPERS FORM THE BASIS OF THIS CLASSIC, CHILLED SOUP. ADD A SPOONFUL OF CHUNKY, FRESH AVOCADO SALSA AND A SCATTERING OF CROÛTONS, AND SERVE FOR A LIGHT LUNCH OR SIMPLE SUPPER ON A WARM SUMMER DAY.

SERVES FOUR

INGREDIENTS

- 2 slices day-old white bread, cubed
- 600ml/1 pint/2½ cups chilled water
- 1kg/2¼lb tomatoes
- 1 cucumber
- 1 red (bell) pepper, halved, seeded and chopped
- 1 fresh green chilli, seeded and chopped
- 2 garlic cloves, chopped
- 30ml/2 tbsp extra virgin olive oil
- juice of 1 lime and 1 lemon
- a few drops of Tabasco sauce
- salt and ground black pepper
- 8 ice cubes, to garnish
- a handful of basil leaves, to garnish

For the croûtons

- 2 slices day-old bread, crusts removed
- 1 garlic clove, halved
- 15ml/1 tbsp olive oil

For the avocado salsa

- 1 ripe avocado
- 5ml/1 tsp lemon juice
- 2.5cm/1in piece cucumber, diced
- ½ red chilli, seeded and finely chopped

1 Place the bread in a large bowl and pour over 150ml/¼pint/⅔ cup of the water. Leave to soak for 5 minutes.

2 Meanwhile, place the tomatoes in a bowl and cover with boiling water. Leave for 30 seconds, then peel off the skin, remove the seeds and finely chop the flesh.

3 Thinly peel the cucumber, then cut it in half lengthways and scoop out the seeds with a teaspoon. Discard the inner part and chop the flesh.

4 Place the bread, tomatoes, cucumber, red pepper, chilli, garlic, olive oil, citrus juices and Tabasco in a food processor or blender with the remaining 450ml/¾ pint/scant 2 cups chilled water and blend until well combined but still chunky. Season to taste and chill for 2–3 hours.

5 To make the croûtons, rub the slices of bread with the garlic clove. Cut the bread into cubes and place in a plastic bag with the olive oil. Seal the bag and shake until the bread cubes are coated with the oil.

6 Heat a large non-stick frying pan and fry the croûtons over a medium heat until crisp and golden.

7 Just before serving, make the avocado salsa. Halve the avocado, remove the stone (pit), then peel and dice. Toss the avocado in the lemon juice to prevent it from browning, then place it in a serving bowl and add the cucumber and chilli. Mix well.

8 Ladle the soup into four chilled bowls and add a couple of ice cubes to each. Top each portion with a good spoonful of avocado salsa. Garnish with the basil and sprinkle the croûtons over the top of the salsa.

FRESH TOMATO SOUP

THE COMBINATION OF INTENSELY FLAVOURED SUN-RIPENED AND FRESH TOMATOES NEEDS LITTLE EMBELLISHMENT IN THIS TASTY ITALIAN SOUP. CHOOSE THE RIPEST-LOOKING TOMATOES AND ADD SUGAR AND BALSAMIC VINEGAR TO TASTE. THE QUANTITY WILL DEPEND ON THE NATURAL SWEETNESS OF THE FRESH TOMATOES. ON A HOT DAY, THIS SOUP IS ALSO DELICIOUS CHILLED.

SERVES SIX

INGREDIENTS

1.3–1.6kg/3–3½lb ripe tomatoes
400ml/14fl oz/1⅔ cups chicken or
   vegetable stock
45ml/3 tbsp sun-dried tomato
   purée (paste)
30–45ml/2–3 tbsp balsamic vinegar
10–15ml/2–3 tsp sugar
a small handful of fresh basil leaves,
   plus extra to garnish
salt and ground black pepper
toasted cheese croûtes and crème
   fraîche, to serve

COOK'S TIP
Use a sharp knife to cut a cross in the base of each tomato before plunging it into the boiling water. The skin will then peel back easily from the crosses.

1 Plunge the tomatoes into boiling water for 30 seconds, then refresh in cold water. Peel off the skins and quarter the tomatoes. Put them in a large pan and pour over the chicken or vegetable stock. Bring just to the boil, reduce the heat, cover and simmer gently for 10 minutes until the tomatoes are pulpy.

2 Stir in the tomato purée, vinegar, sugar and basil. Season with salt and pepper, then cook gently, stirring, for 2 minutes. Process the soup in a blender or food processor, then return to a clean pan and reheat gently. Serve in bowls, topped with one or two toasted cheese croûtes and a spoonful of crème fraîche, garnished with basil leaves.

FRAGRANT TOMATO SOUP

ALTHOUGH BASIL IS TRADITIONALLY USED TO PARTNER TOMATOES, FRESH CORIANDER ALSO COMPLEMENTS THEIR FLAVOUR. THIS WARMING SOUP IS EXCELLENT ON A COLD WINTER'S DAY.

3 Add the salt, garlic, peppercorns and fresh coriander to the tomato mixture. Add the water and bring to the boil, lower the heat and simmer for 15–20 minutes.

4 Dissolve the cornflour in a little cold water. Remove the soup from the heat and press it through a sieve.

5 Return the soup to a clean pan, add the cornflour paste and stir over a very gentle heat for about 3 minutes or so until thickened. Pour the soup into individual serving dishes and garnish each serving with a swirl of cream. Serve immediately.

SERVES FOUR

INGREDIENTS

675g/1½lb tomatoes
30ml/2 tbsp vegetable oil
1 bay leaf
4 spring onions (scallions), chopped
5ml/1 tsp salt
1 garlic clove, crushed
5ml/1 tsp black peppercorns, crushed
30ml/2 tbsp chopped fresh
  coriander (cilantro)
750ml/1¼ pints/3 cups water
15ml/1 tbsp cornflour (cornstarch)
30ml/2 tbsp single (light) cream,
  to garnish

COOK'S TIP
In winter when fresh tomatoes can be rather pale and under-ripe, add 15ml/ 1 tbsp tomato purée (paste).

1 Plunge the tomatoes into boiling water for 30 seconds, then refresh in cold water. Peel away the skins and chop the tomatoes.

2 In a medium pan, heat the oil and fry the chopped tomatoes, bay leaf and spring onions for a few minutes until the spring onions are soft and the tomatoes have cooked down a little.

SUMMER VEGETABLE SOUP

THIS BRIGHTLY COLOURED, FRESH-TASTING TOMATO SOUP MAKES THE MOST OF SUMMER VEGETABLES IN SEASON. ADD LOTS OF RED AND YELLOW PEPPERS TO MAKE A SWEETER VERSION.

SERVES FOUR

INGREDIENTS

  450g/1lb ripe plum tomatoes
  225g/8oz ripe yellow tomatoes
  45ml/3 tbsp olive oil
  1 large onion, finely chopped
  15ml/1 tbsp sun-dried tomato
    purée (paste)
  225g/8oz green courgettes (summer
    squash), trimmed and roughly chopped
  225g/8oz yellow courgettes, trimmed
    and roughly chopped
  3 waxy new potatoes, diced
  2 garlic cloves, crushed
  about 1.2 litres/2 pints/5 cups
    chicken stock or water
  60ml/4 tbsp shredded fresh basil
  50g/2oz/⅔ cup freshly grated
    (shredded) Parmesan cheese
  sea salt and freshly ground
    black pepper

1 Plunge all the tomatoes in boiling water for 30 seconds, refresh in cold water, then peel and chop finely. Heat the oil in a large pan, add the onion and cook gently for about 5 minutes, stirring constantly, until softened. Stir in the sun-dried tomato purée, chopped tomatoes, courgettes, diced potatoes and garlic. Mix well and cook gently for 10 minutes, shaking the pan often.

2 Pour in the stock or water. Bring to the boil, lower the heat, half cover the pan and simmer gently for 15 minutes or until the vegetables are just tender. Add more stock or water if necessary.

3 Remove the pan from the heat and stir in the basil and half the cheese. Taste for seasoning. Serve hot, sprinkled with the remaining cheese.

ONION <u>AND</u> TOMATO SOUP

THIS WARMING WINTER SOUP COMES FROM UMBRIA, IN ITALY, WHERE IT WAS TRADITIONALLY THICKENED WITH BEATEN EGGS AND LOTS OF GRATED PARMESAN CHEESE. IT WAS THEN SERVED ON TOP OF HOT TOASTED CROÛTES — RATHER LIKE SAVOURY SCRAMBLED EGGS.

SERVES FOUR

INGREDIENTS

115g/4oz pancetta, rind removed,
  roughly chopped
30ml/2 tbsp olive oil
15g/½oz/1 tbsp butter
675g/1½lb onions, thinly sliced
10ml/2 tsp granulated sugar
350g/12oz ripe plum tomatoes
about 1.2 litres/2 pints/5 cups
  chicken stock
a few fresh basil leaves, shredded
salt and ground black pepper
ciabatta and a chunk of Parmesan
  cheese, to serve

1 Put the chopped pancetta in a large pan and heat gently, stirring constantly, until the fat runs. Increase the heat to medium, add the oil, butter, onions and sugar, and stir well to mix.

2 Half cover the pan and cook the onions gently for about 20 minutes until golden. Lift the lid and stir frequently, lowering the heat if necessary.

3 Plunge the tomatoes into boiling water for 30 seconds, refresh in cold water, drain and peel.

4 Chop the tomatoes and add to the pan with the stock. Add salt and pepper and bring to the boil, stirring. Lower the heat, half cover the pan and simmer, stirring occasionally, for about 30 minutes.

5 Check the consistency of the soup and add a little more stock or water if it is too thick.

6 Just before serving, stir in most of the basil and taste for seasoning. Serve hot, garnished with the remaining basil. Serve with ciabatta and invite guests to grate in their own Parmesan.

COOK'S TIPS
• Beefsteak tomatoes are good in this soup as they are very fleshy with few seeds. You could try adding a few whole cherry tomatoes just before the end of the cooking time, which will add an interesting look to the dish.
• Look for Vidalia onions to make this soup. They are often available at large supermarkets, and have a very sweet, mild flavour and attractive yellowish flesh.

TORTILLA TOMATO SOUP

THERE ARE SEVERAL TORTILLA SOUPS. THIS ONE IS AN AGUADA – OR LIQUID – VERSION, AND IS INTENDED FOR SERVING AS AN APPETIZER OR LIGHT MEAL. IT IS VERY EASY AND QUICK TO PREPARE, OR MAKE IT IN ADVANCE AND FRY THE TORTILLA STRIPS AS IT REHEATS. THE CRISP TORTILLA PIECES ADD INTEREST AND GIVE THE SOUP AN UNUSUAL TEXTURE.

SERVES FOUR

INGREDIENTS
    4 corn tortillas
    15ml/1 tbsp vegetable oil, plus extra,
      for frying
    1 small onion, chopped
    2 garlic cloves, crushed
    350g/12oz ripe plum tomatoes
    400g/14oz can plum tomatoes, drained
    1 litre/1¾ pints/4 cups chicken stock
    small bunch of fresh coriander (cilantro)
    50g/2oz/½ cup grated (shredded)
      mild Cheddar cheese
    salt and ground black pepper

1 Using a sharp knife, cut each tortilla into four or five strips, each measuring about 2cm/¾in wide. Pour vegetable oil to a depth of 2cm/¾in into a frying pan. Heat until a small piece of tortilla, added to the oil, floats on the top and bubbles at the edges.

2 Add a few tortilla strips to the hot oil and fry until crisp and golden brown.

3 Remove the tortilla chips with a slotted spoon and drain on kitchen paper. Cook the remaining tortilla strips in the same way.

4 Heat the 15ml/1 tbsp vegetable oil in a large pan. Add the onion and garlic and cook over a medium heat for 2–3 minutes, until the onion is soft and translucent. Do not let the garlic turn brown or it will give the soup a bitter taste.

5 Skin the fresh tomatoes by plunging them into boiling water for 30 seconds, refreshing them in cold water, draining them and then peeling off the skins with a sharp knife.

6 Chop the fresh and canned tomatoes and add them to the onion mixture. Pour in the chicken stock. Bring to the boil, then lower the heat and allow to simmer for approximately 10 minutes, until the liquid has reduced slightly. Stir occasionally.

7 Roughly chop or tear the coriander into pieces. Add it to the soup and season with salt and ground black pepper to taste.

8 Place a few of the crisp tortilla pieces in each of four large heated soup bowls. Ladle the soup on top. Sprinkle each portion with some of the grated mild Cheddar cheese and serve immediately.

COOK'S TIP
An easy way to chop fresh herbs is to put them in a mug and snip with a pair of scissors. Hold the scissors vertically with one hand on each handle and work the blades back and forth until the herbs are finely and evenly chopped. If you are using woody herbs, such as rosemary or thyme, remember to strip the leaves from the stalks before putting them in the mug. They are then ready to be chopped.

EGG-STUFFED TOMATOES

THIS SIMPLE DISH IS JUST THE KIND OF THING YOU MIGHT FIND IN A CHARCUTERIE IN FRANCE.
IT IS EASY TO MAKE AT HOME AND MAKES A DELICIOUS APPETIZER OR A LIGHT LUNCH.

SERVES FOUR

INGREDIENTS
  175ml/6fl oz/¾ cup mayonnaise
  30ml/2 tbsp chopped fresh chives
  30ml/2 tbsp chopped fresh basil
  30ml/2 tbsp chopped fresh parsley
  4 hard-boiled (hard-cooked) eggs
  4 ripe tomatoes
  salt and ground black pepper
  salad leaves, to serve

1 In a small bowl, mix together the mayonnaise and herbs. Set aside. Using an egg slicer or sharp knife, cut the eggs into thin slices, taking care to keep the slices intact.

2 Make deep cuts to within 1cm/½in of the base of each tomato. (There should be the same number of cuts in each tomato as there are slices of egg.)

3 Fan open the tomatoes and sprinkle with salt, then insert an egg slice into each slit. Place each stuffed tomato on a plate with a few salad leaves, season and serve with the herb mayonnaise.

GRIDDLED TOMATOES ON SODA BREAD

NOTHING COULD BE SIMPLER THAN THIS DISH, YET A DRIZZLE OF OLIVE OIL AND BALSAMIC VINEGAR AND SHAVINGS OF PARMESAN CHEESE TRANSFORM TOMATOES ON TOAST INTO SOMETHING REALLY SPECIAL.

SERVES FOUR

INGREDIENTS
olive oil, for brushing and drizzling
6 tomatoes, thickly sliced
4 thick slices soda bread
balsamic vinegar, for drizzling
salt and ground black pepper
shavings of Parmesan cheese,
 to serve

VARIATIONS
• For a more substantial meal, place a couple of slices of prosciutto on the toast before adding the tomatoes.
• This recipe is also delicious with slices of mozzarella cheese instead of the shaved Parmesan.
• Anchovies go well with tomatoes. If you like them, try tearing a few anchovy fillets into strips and arranging them on top of the tomatoes. Omit the Parmesan.

1 Brush a griddle pan with a little olive oil and heat. Add the tomato slices and cook for about 4 minutes, turning once, until softened and slightly blackened. Alternatively, heat a grill (broiler) to high and line the rack with foil. Grill (broil) the tomato slices for 4–6 minutes, turning once, until softened.

2 Meanwhile, lightly toast the soda bread until pale golden.

3 Place the tomatoes on top of the toast and drizzle each portion with a little olive oil and balsamic vinegar. Season with salt and ground black pepper to taste and serve immediately with thin shavings of Parmesan.

COOK'S TIP
Using a griddle pan reduces the amount of oil required for cooking the tomatoes and gives them a barbecued flavour.

TOASTED CIABATTA WITH TOMATOES, CHEESE AND MARJORAM FLOWERS

HERE IS A VERY SIMPLE BUT TASTY METHOD OF USING MARJORAM FLOWERS. THE COMBINATION OF CHEESE, TOMATO AND MARJORAM IS POPULAR, BUT LOTS OF EXTRAS CAN BE ADDED, SUCH AS CAPERS, OLIVES, ANCHOVIES OR SLICES OF ROASTED PEPPERS.

SERVES TWO

INGREDIENTS

1 ciabatta loaf
4 tomatoes
115g/4oz mozzarella or
 Cheddar cheese
15ml/1 tbsp olive oil
15ml/1 tbsp marjoram flowers
salt and ground black pepper

COOK'S TIP
Add marjoram flowers to your favourite pizza topping. Sprinkle over 7.5–15ml/ ½–1 tbsp flowers or flowering tops and add a few of the leaves. The flavours are strong, so marjoram flowers should be used with care, especially if you haven't tried them before. The amount you use will depend on your own palate.

1 Preheat the grill (broiler) to high. Cut the loaf in half lengthwise and toast very lightly under the grill until it has turned a pale golden brown.

2 Meanwhile, skin the tomatoes by plunging them in boiling water for 30 seconds, then refreshing them in cold water. Peel and cut into thick slices.

3 Slice or grate the cheese. Lightly drizzle the olive oil over the bread and top with the tomato slices and sliced or grated cheese. Season with salt and pepper and scatter the marjoram flowers over the top. Drizzle with a little more olive oil. Return to the grill until the cheese bubbles and is just starting to brown.

CROSTINI WITH TOMATO AND VEGETABLE TOPPING

THIS POPULAR ITALIAN HORS D'OEUVRE WAS ORIGINALLY A WAY OF USING UP LEFTOVERS AND THE OVERABUNDANCE OF TOMATOES FROM THE HARVEST. PLUM TOMATOES ARE TRADITIONALLY USED, BUT CHERRY TOMATOES ARE A DELICIOUS ALTERNATIVE.

MAKES SIXTEEN

INGREDIENTS

1 ciabatta or French loaf
For the tomato, (bell) pepper and anchovy topping
  400g/14oz can or bottle Italian
    roasted red (bell) peppers
    and tomatoes
  50g/2oz can anchovy fillets
  extra virgin olive oil, for drizzling
  15–30ml/1–2 tbsp balsamic vinegar
  1 garlic clove
  red pesto, for brushing
  30ml/2 tbsp chopped fresh chives,
    oregano or sage, to garnish
  15ml/1 tbsp capers, to garnish
For the mozzarella and tomato topping
  green pesto sauce, for brushing
  120ml/4fl oz/½ cup thick home-made
    or bottled tomato sauce or
    pizza topping
  115g/4oz good quality mozzarella
    cheese, cut into thin slices
  2–3 ripe plum tomatoes, seeded and
    cut into strips
  fresh basil leaves, to garnish

COOK'S TIP
For an extra healthy version, use wholemeal (whole-wheat) toast instead of a ciabatta loaf.

1 Cut the ciabatta or French bread into 16 slices. Toast until crisp and golden on both sides. Cool on a wire rack.

2 For the tomato, pepper and anchovy topping, drain the tomatoes and peppers and wipe dry with kitchen paper. Cut into 1 cm/½in strips and place in a shallow dish.

3 Rinse and dry the anchovy fillets and add to the peppers and tomatoes. Drizzle with olive oil and sprinkle with the balsamic vinegar.

4 Using a sharp knife peel and halve the garlic clove. Rub 8 toasts with the cut edge of the clove and brush the toast with a little red pesto. Arrange the tomatoes, peppers and anchovies decoratively on the toasts and sprinkle with herbs and capers.

5 For the mozzarella and tomato topping, brush the remaining toasts with the green pesto and spoon on some tomato sauce. Arrange a slice of mozzarella on each and cover with the tomato strips. Garnish with basil leaves.

BAKED POLENTA <u>WITH</u> TOMATOES

THESE HERB-FLAVOURED POLENTA SQUARES INTERLEAVED WITH TOMATO AND TOPPED WITH CHEESE ARE AN EASY VERSION OF PIZZA! THE IMPORTANT THING TO REMEMBER IS TO ALLOW TIME FOR THE POLENTA TO COOL AND SET, BEFORE CUTTING AND TOPPING IT.

SERVES SIX

INGREDIENTS

750ml/1¼ pints/3 cups chicken or
  vegetable stock
175g/6oz/1 cup polenta
60ml/4 tbsp finely chopped
  fresh sage
15ml/1 tbsp extra virgin olive oil,
  for greasing
3 beefsteak tomatoes,
  thinly sliced
15ml/1 tbsp freshly grated
  (shredded) Parmesan cheese
salt and ground black pepper

1 Bring the stock to the boil in a large pan, then gradually stir in the polenta, using a wooden spoon.

2 Continue stirring the polenta over a medium heat for about 5 minutes, until the mixture begins to come away from the sides of the pan.

3 Stir in the chopped sage and season well, then spoon into a lightly oiled, shallow 33 x 23cm/13 x 9in tray and spread evenly. Leave to cool.

4 Preheat the oven to 200°C/400°F/Gas 6. Cut the cooled polenta into 24 squares, using a sharp knife.

5 Arrange the polenta squares in a lightly oiled, shallow ovenproof dish, slipping a slice of tomato between each square. Sprinkle with Parmesan and bake for 20 minutes or until golden brown. Serve hot.

COOK'S TIP
If you dip the knife in a jug of boiling water from time to time, the polenta will be easier to cut.

BAKED VEGETABLE SLICES <u>WITH</u> CHEESE

IN THE PAST, IT WAS NECESSARY TO SALT AUBERGINES TO DRAW OUT THEIR BITTERNESS, BUT THIS IS NO LONGER NECESSARY, THANKS TO THE DEVELOPMENT OF MILDER EXAMPLES THAT ARE SOLD WHEN THEY ARE YOUNG AND TENDER. TODAY, THEY CAN BE SLICED AND USED IMMEDIATELY, AS IN THIS TASTY DISH.

SERVES FOUR

INGREDIENTS

  45–60ml/3–4 tbsp olive oil,
    for brushing
  1 large aubergine (eggplant)
  1 large or 2 medium tomatoes,
    thickly sliced
  a few fresh basil leaves, shredded
  115g/4oz mozzarella cheese, sliced
  salt and ground black pepper
  fresh basil, to garnish

COOK'S TIP
These aubergine slices are substantial enough to be served as a light lunch, or as part of a vegetarian meal.

1 Preheat the oven to 190°C/375°F/ Gas 5. Brush a baking sheet with a little oil. Trim the aubergine and cut it lengthways into four slices about 5mm/ ¼in thick. Arrange the slices on the greased baking sheet.

2 Brush the aubergine slices liberally with oil and sprinkle with seasoning.

3 Arrange about three or four tomato slices on top of each aubergine slice, overlapping them slightly, if necessary. Sprinkle over about half of the shredded basil.

4 Top with the cheese or interleave it with the tomato. Brush with more oil. Bake for 15 minutes, or until the aubergine is tender and the cheese is bubbling. Garnish and serve.

The concentrated flavour of tomatoes adds a delicious richness to any sauce. Whether included in a main dish or as part of an accompanying sauce, the unique taste and texture of tomatoes is always popular. They are one of the most versatile ingredients to incorporate into main dishes, and can be used in a variety of ways — whole, as in Romanian Kebabs; sliced, as in Polpettes with Mozzarella and Tomato; or peeled and chopped, as in Clams with Neapolitan Tomato Sauce.

Main Meals

CLAMS WITH NEAPOLITAN TOMATO SAUCE

THIS RECIPE TAKES ITS NAME FROM THE CITY OF NAPLES, WHERE BOTH FRESH TOMATO SAUCE AND SHELLFISH ARE TRADITIONALLY SERVED WITH VERMICELLI. HERE THE TWO ARE COMBINED TO MAKE A VERY TASTY DISH THAT IS PERFECT FOR A COLD WINTER'S EVENING.

SERVES FOUR

INGREDIENTS

1kg/2¼lb fresh clams
250ml/8fl oz/1 cup dry white wine,
  or vegetable stock
2 garlic cloves, bruised
1 large handful fresh flat leaf parsley
30ml/2 tbsp extra virgin olive oil or
  sunflower oil
1 small onion, finely chopped
8 ripe plum tomatoes, peeled, seeded
  and finely chopped
½–1 fresh red chilli, seeded and
  finely chopped
350g/12oz dried vermicelli
salt and ground black pepper

1 Scrub the clams thoroughly with a brush under cold running water and discard any that are open or do not close their shells when sharply tapped against the work surface.

2 Pour the white wine or vegetable stock into a large, heavy pan and add the bruised garlic cloves. Shred half the parsley finely, then add to the wine or stock, then add the clams.

3 Cover the pan tightly with the lid and bring to the boil over a high heat. Cook for about 5 minutes, shaking the pan frequently, until all the clams have re-opened.

4 Tip the clams into a large colander set over a bowl and let the liquid drain through. Leave the clams until cool enough to handle, then remove about two-thirds of them from their shells, tipping the clam liquor into the bowl of cooking liquid.

5 Discard any clams that have failed to open. Set both shelled and unshelled clams aside, keeping the unshelled clams warm in a bowl covered with a lid or thick cloth.

6 Heat the oil in a pan, add the onion and cook gently, stirring frequently, for about 5 minutes until softened and lightly coloured. Add the tomatoes, then strain in the clam cooking liquid. Add the chilli, and salt and pepper to taste.

7 Bring to the boil, half cover the pan and simmer gently for 15–20 minutes. Meanwhile, cook the pasta according to the packet instructions. Chop the remaining parsley finely.

8 Add the shelled clams to the tomato sauce, stir well and heat through very gently for 2–3 minutes.

9 Drain the cooked pasta well and tip it into a warmed bowl. Taste the sauce for seasoning, then pour the sauce over the pasta and toss everything together well. Garnish with the reserved clams, sprinkle the parsley over the pasta and serve immediately.

PASTA <u>WITH</u> TOMATOES <u>AND</u> SHELLFISH

COLOURFUL AND DELICIOUS, THIS TYPICAL GENOESE DISH IS IDEAL FOR A DINNER PARTY. THE TOMATO SAUCE IS QUITE RUNNY, SO SERVE IT WITH CRUSTY BREAD AND SPOONS AS WELL AS FORKS. FOR A REAL TASTE OF ITALY, CHOOSE A DRY WHITE ITALIAN WINE TO SERVE WITH THE MEAL.

SERVES FOUR

INGREDIENTS

45ml/3 tbsp olive oil
1 small onion, chopped
1 garlic clove, crushed
½ fresh red chilli, seeded
  and chopped
200g/7oz can chopped
  plum tomatoes
30ml/2 tbsp chopped fresh flat
  leaf parsley
400g/14oz fresh clams
400g/14oz fresh mussels
60ml/4 tbsp dry white wine
400g/14oz/3½ cups dried trenette
  or spaghetti
a few fresh basil leaves
90g/3½oz/⅔ cup cooked, peeled
  prawns (shrimp), thawed and
  thoroughly dried if frozen
salt and ground black pepper
lemon wedges and chopped fresh herbs,
  such as parsley or thyme, to garnish

1 Heat 30ml/2tbsp of the oil in a frying pan or medium pan. Add the onion, garlic and chilli, and cook over a medium heat for 1–2 minutes, stirring constantly. Stir in the tomatoes, half the parsley and pepper to taste. Bring to the boil, lower the heat, cover and simmer for 15 minutes.

2 Meanwhile, scrub the clams and mussels under cold running water. Discard any that are open and that do not close when sharply tapped against the work surface.

3 In a large pan, heat the remaining oil. Add the clams and mussels, with the rest of the parsley and toss over a high heat for a few seconds. Pour in the wine, then cover tightly. Cook for about 5 minutes, shaking the pan frequently, until the clams and mussels have opened.

4 Transfer the clams and mussels to a bowl, discarding any shellfish that have failed to open. Strain the cooking liquid and set aside. Reserve 8 clams and 4 mussels for the garnish, then remove the rest from their shells.

5 Cook the pasta according to the instructions on the packet. Meanwhile, add 120ml/4fl oz/ ½ cup of the reserved shellfish liquid to the tomato sauce. Add the basil, prawns, shelled clams and mussels to the sauce. Season.

6 Drain the pasta and tip it into a warmed bowl. Add the sauce and toss well to combine. Serve in individual bowls, sprinkle with herbs and garnish each portion with lemon, 2 clams and 1 mussel in their shells.

PRAWNS WITH ALMOND AND TOMATO SAUCE

GROUND ALMONDS ADD AN INTERESTING TEXTURE TO THE CREAMY, PIQUANT SAUCE THAT ACCOMPANIES THESE SUCCULENT SHELLFISH.

SERVES SIX

INGREDIENTS
   1 dried chilli
   1 onion
   3 garlic cloves
   30ml/2 tbsp vegetable oil
   8 plum tomatoes
   5ml/1 tsp ground cumin
   120ml/4fl oz/½ cup chicken stock
   130g/4½oz/generous 1 cup
     ground almonds
   175ml/6fl oz/¾ cup crème fraîche
   ½ lime
   900g/2lb cooked, peeled
     prawns (shrimp)
   salt
   fresh coriander (cilantro) and spring
     onion (scallion) strips, to garnish
   cooked rice and warm tortillas,
     to serve

VARIATION
Try this sauce with other types of fish. Adding just a few prawns and serving it over steamed sole makes a very luxurious dish.

1 Place the dried chilli in a heatproof bowl and pour over boiling water to cover. Leave to soak for 30 minutes until softened. Drain, remove the stalk, then slit the chilli and scrape out the seeds with a small sharp knife. Chop the flesh roughly and set it aside.

2 Chop the onion finely and then crush the cloves of garlic. Heat the oil in a frying pan and fry the onion and garlic over a low heat until soft.

3 Cut a cross in the base of each tomato. Place them in a heatproof bowl and cover with boiling water. After 30 seconds, lift them out and plunge them into a bowl of cold water. Drain.

4 Skin and seed the tomatoes. Chop the flesh into 1cm/½in cubes and add them to the onion mixture in the frying pan, with the chopped chilli. Stir in the ground cumin and cook for 10 minutes, stirring occasionally.

5 Tip the mixture into a food processor or blender. Add the stock and process on high speed until smooth.

6 Pour the mixture into a large pan, then add the ground almonds and stir over a low heat for 2–3 minutes. Stir in the crème fraîche until it has been incorporated completely.

7 Squeeze the juice from the lime into the sauce and stir it in. Season with salt to taste, then increase the heat and bring the sauce to simmering point.

8 Add the prawns to the sauce and heat until warmed through. Serve on a bed of hot rice garnished with the coriander and spring onion strips. Offer warm tortillas separately.

SALMON AND TUNA PARCELS

YOU NEED FAIRLY LARGE SMOKED SALMON SLICES FOR THIS DISH, AS THEY ARE WRAPPED AROUND A
LIGHT TUNA MIXTURE BEFORE BEING SERVED ON A VIBRANT TOMATO SALAD.

SERVES FOUR

INGREDIENTS
   30ml/2 tbsp natural (plain) yogurt
   15ml/1 tbsp tomato purée (paste)
   5ml/1 tsp wholegrain honey mustard
   grated rind and juice of 1 lime
   200g/7oz can tuna in brine, drained
   12–16 large slices of smoked salmon
   salt and ground black pepper
   fresh mint leaves, to garnish
For the salad
   3 ripe vine tomatoes, sliced
   2 kiwi fruit, peeled and sliced
   ¼ cucumber, cut into julienne sticks
   15ml/1 tbsp chopped fresh mint
   7.5ml/1½ tsp white wine vinegar
   45ml/3 tbsp olive oil
   2.5ml/½ tsp mustard

1 Mix the yogurt, tomato purée and mustard in a bowl. Stir in the grated lime rind and juice. Add the tuna, with black pepper to taste, and mix well.

2 Spread out the salmon slices on a chopping board and spoon some of the tuna mixture on to each piece.

3 Roll up or fold the smoked salmon into neat parcels. Carefully press the edges together to seal.

COOK'S TIP
Whole sides of smoked salmon are often on sale quite cheaply around Christmas time, and would be ideal. As the filling is strongly flavoured, it is quite all right to use farmed salmon. The parcels would make a welcome change from turkey.

4 Make the salad. Arrange the tomato and kiwi slices on 4 serving plates. Sprinkle over the cucumber sticks. In a bowl, whisk the chopped mint, white wine vinegar, oil, mustard and a little seasoning together and spoon some over each salad.

5 Arrange 3–4 salmon parcels on each plate, garnish with the fresh mint leaves and serve immediately.

COD PLAKI

GENERALLY, FISH IS SERVED VERY SIMPLY IN GREECE, BUT THIS TRADITIONAL RECIPE IS A LITTLE MORE ELABORATE, AND INVOLVES BRAISING THE FISH WITH TOMATOES AND ONIONS.

SERVES SIX

INGREDIENTS

300ml/½ pint/1¼ cups extra virgin olive oil
2 onions, thinly sliced
6 large well-flavoured tomatoes, roughly chopped
3 garlic cloves, thinly sliced
5ml/1 tsp granulated sugar
5ml/1 tsp chopped fresh dill
5ml/1 tsp chopped fresh mint
5ml/1 tsp chopped fresh celery leaves
15ml/1 tbsp chopped fresh parsley
6 cod steaks, about 175g/6oz each
juice of 1 lemon
salt and ground black pepper
extra dill, mint or parsley, or other fresh herbs, to garnish

1 Heat the oil in a large sauté pan or flameproof casserole. Add the onions and cook until pale golden. Add the tomatoes, garlic, sugar, chopped dill, mint, celery leaves and parsley with 300ml/ ½ pint/1¼ cups water. Season with salt and pepper, then simmer, uncovered, for 25 minutes, until the liquid has reduced by one-third.

2 Add the fish steaks to the pan or casserole and braise gently for 10–12 minutes, until the fish is just cooked. Remove from the heat and add the lemon juice. Cover and leave to stand for about 20 minutes before serving. Arrange the cod in a dish and spoon the sauce over. Garnish with herbs and serve warm or cold.

BAKED FISH WITH TAHINI SAUCE

THIS AFRICAN RECIPE EVOKES ALL THE COLOUR AND RICH FLAVOURS OF THE SUN. ALTHOUGH THE TOMATOES ARE PRESENTED VERY SIMPLY HERE, THEY ARE AN ESSENTIAL ADDITION.

SERVES FOUR

INGREDIENTS
   1 whole white fish, about
     1.2kg/2½lb, scaled and cleaned
   10ml/2 tsp coriander seeds
   4 garlic cloves, sliced
   10ml/2 tsp harissa
   90ml/6 tbsp olive oil
   18 plum tomatoes, sliced
   1 onion, sliced
   3 preserved lemons or 1 fresh lemon
   plenty of fresh herbs, such as bay
     leaves, thyme and rosemary
   salt and ground black pepper
   extra herbs, to garnish
For the sauce
   75ml/5 tbsp light tahini sauce
   juice of 1 lemon
   1 garlic clove, crushed
   45ml/3 tbsp finely chopped fresh
     parsley or coriander (cilantro)

1 Preheat the oven to 200°C/400°F/ Gas 6. Grease the base and sides of a large shallow ovenproof dish or roasting pan that will hold the fish.

2 Slash the fish diagonally on both sides with a sharp knife. Finely crush the coriander seeds and garlic with a pestle and mortar. Mix with the harissa and about 60ml/4 tbsp of the olive oil.

3 Spread a little of the harissa, coriander and garlic paste inside the cavity of the fish, then spread the remainder over each side of the fish and set aside.

4 Scatter the tomatoes, onion and preserved or fresh lemon into the dish or pan. (Thinly slice the lemon if using fresh.) Sprinkle with the remaining oil and season with salt and pepper. Lay the fish on top and tuck plenty of herbs around it. Bake, uncovered, for about 25 minutes, or until the flesh of the fish has turned opaque – test by piercing the thickest part with a knife.

5 Meanwhile, make the sauce. Put the tahini, lemon juice, garlic and parsley or coriander in a small pan with 120ml/ 4fl oz/½ cup water. Stir in a little salt and pepper. Heat through gently and serve in a separate dish.

COOK'S TIP
If you can't get a suitable large fish, use several small fish, such as red mullet or snapper. Reduce the cooking time slightly.

RED SNAPPER WITH CHILLIES AND TOMATOES

THIS COLOURFUL DISH COMBINES BAY LEAVES AND OLIVES WITH FRESH GREEN CHILLIES IN A RICH TOMATO SAUCE.

SERVES FOUR

INGREDIENTS
    4 whole red snapper, cleaned
    juice of 2 limes
    4 garlic cloves, crushed
    5ml/1 tsp dried oregano
    2.5ml/½ tsp salt
    drained bottled capers, to garnish
    lime wedges, to serve (optional)
    lime rind, to garnish
For the sauce
    120ml/4fl oz/½ cup olive oil
    2 bay leaves
    2 garlic cloves, sliced
    4 fresh chillies, seeded and cut
      in strips
    1 onion, thinly sliced
    450g/1lb fresh tomatoes
    75g/3oz/½ cup pickled jalapeño
      chilli slices
    15ml/1 tbsp soft dark brown sugar
    2.5ml/½ tsp ground cloves
    2.5ml/½ tsp ground cinnamon
    150g/5oz/1¼ cups green olives
      stuffed with pimiento

4 Add the onion slices to the flavoured oil in the pan and cook for 3–4 minutes more, until all the onion is softened and translucent. Keep the heat low and stir the onions often so that they do not brown.

5 Cut a cross in the base of each tomato. Place them in a heatproof bowl and pour over boiling water to cover. After 30 seconds, lift the tomatoes out on a slotted spoon and plunge them into a bowl of cold water. Drain. The skins will have begun to peel back from the crosses.

6 Skin the tomatoes completely, then cut them in half and squeeze out the seeds. Chop the flesh finely and add it to the onion. Cook for 3–4 minutes, until the tomato is starting to soften.

7 Add the pickled jalapeños, brown sugar, ground cloves and cinnamon to the sauce. Cook for 10 minutes, stirring frequently, then stir the olives into the sauce and pour a little over each fish. Garnish with the capers and lime rind and serve with lime wedges for squeezing over the fish, if you like. A rice dish would make a good accompaniment.

1 Preheat the oven to 180°C/350°F/ Gas 4. Rinse the fish inside and out. Pat dry with kitchen paper. Place in a large roasting pan in a single layer.

2 Mix the lime juice, garlic, oregano and salt. Pour the mixture over the fish. Bake for about 30 minutes, or until the flesh flakes easily.

3 Make the sauce. Heat the oil in a pan, add the bay leaves, garlic and chilli strips; fry for 3–4 minutes.

TURKISH COLD FISH <u>WITH</u> TOMATOES

COLD FISH DISHES ARE MUCH APPRECIATED IN THE MIDDLE EAST AND FOR GOOD REASON – THEY ARE DELICIOUS! THE TOMATO TOPPING GIVES A WONDERFUL COLOUR TO THIS MEAL.

SERVES FOUR

INGREDIENTS
    60ml/4 tbsp extra virgin olive oil, or
        sunflower oil
    900g/2lb red mullet or snapper
    2 onions, sliced
    1 green (bell) pepper, seeded and sliced
    1 red (bell) pepper, seeded and sliced
    3 garlic cloves, crushed
    15ml/1 tbsp tomato purée (paste)
    60ml/4 tbsp fish stock or water
    5–6 tomatoes, peeled and sliced
    400g/14oz can tomatoes
    30ml/2 tbsp chopped fresh parsley
    30ml/2 tbsp lemon juice
    5ml/1 tsp paprika
    15–20 green and black olives
    salt and ground black pepper
    bread and salad, to serve

VARIATION
One large fish looks spectacular, but it is tricky to both cook and serve. If you prefer, buy 4 smaller fish or fish steaks and cook for a shorter time, until just tender. The flesh should flake when tested with the tip of a knife.

1 Heat half the oil in a large roasting pan and fry the fish on both sides until golden brown. Remove from the pan, cover and keep warm.

COOK'S TIP
The delicate flesh of red mullet is highly perishable, so it is important to buy fish that is absolutely fresh, and cook it as soon as possible after purchase. Ask the fishmonger to scale and gut it for you.

2 Heat the remaining oil in the pan and fry the onions for 2–3 minutes. Add the peppers and cook for 3–4 minutes, stirring occasionally, then add the garlic and stir-fry for 1 minute more.

3 Mix the tomato purée with the fish stock or water and stir into the pan with the fresh and canned tomatoes, parsley, lemon juice, paprika and seasoning. Simmer for 15 minutes.

4 Return the fish to the roasting pan and cover with the sauce. Cook for 10 minutes, then add the olives and cook for a further 5 minutes or until the fish is just cooked through.

5 Transfer the fish to a serving dish and pour the sauce over the top. Allow to cool, then cover and chill until completely cold. Serve cold, with chunks of bread and a mixed salad.

SEA BREAM <u>WITH</u> THYME <u>AND</u> TOMATOES

A WHOLE FISH COATED IN A TANGY LEMON MARINADE IS BAKED ON ROASTED COURGETTES, ONIONS AND TOMATOES UNTIL TENDER AND FLAKY — AN IMPRESSIVE-LOOKING DISH THAT IS EASY TO MAKE AND PERFECT FOR A SPECIAL DINNER PARTY.

<u>SERVES FOUR</u>

INGREDIENTS

   1 or 2 whole sea bream or sea bass,
     total weight 1.3–1.6kg/3–3½lb,
     cleaned and scaled, with the head
     and tail left on
   2 onions
   2 courgettes (zucchini)
   12 tomatoes
   45ml/3 tbsp olive oil
   5ml/1 tsp fresh chopped thyme
   400g/14oz can artichoke hearts
   lemon wedges and finely pared rind,
     black olives and fresh coriander
     (cilantro) leaves, to garnish
For the marinade
   1 onion, chopped
   2 garlic cloves, halved
   ½ bunch fresh parsley
   3–4 fresh coriander (cilantro) sprigs
   pinch of paprika
   45ml/3 tbsp olive oil
   30ml/2 tbsp white wine vinegar
   15ml/1 tbsp lemon juice
   salt and ground black pepper

1 First make the marinade. Place the ingredients in a food processor with 45ml/3 tbsp water and process until the onion is finely chopped and the ingredients are well combined.

2 Make 3–4 slashes on both sides of the fish. Place in a bowl and, using a palette knife (metal spatula), spread with the marinade, pressing it into both sides of the fish. Set aside for 2–3 hours, turning the fish occasionally.

3 Slice the onions. Trim the courgettes and cut into short julienne strips. Peel the tomatoes, discard the seeds and chop roughly.

4 Preheat the oven to 220°C/425°F/Gas 7. Place the onions, courgettes and tomatoes in a shallow ovenproof dish. Sprinkle with the olive oil, salt and thyme, and roast in the oven for 15–20 minutes, until softened and slightly charred, stirring occasionally.

5 Reduce the oven temperature to 180°C/350°F/Gas 4. Drain the artichokes and add them to the dish, spacing them evenly in the vegetable mixture. Place the fish, together with the marinade, on top of the vegetables. Pour over 150ml/¼ pint/⅔ cup water and cover with foil.

6 Bake for 30–35 minutes or until the fish is tender. (Exact timing will depend on whether you are cooking 1 large or 2 smaller fish.) For the last 5 minutes of cooking, remove the foil to allow the skin to brown slightly. Alternatively, if the dish is flameproof, place it under a hot grill (broiler) for 2–3 minutes.

7 Arrange the fish on a large, warmed serving platter and spoon the vegetables around the sides. Garnish with lemon wedges and finely pared strips of rind, black olives and fresh coriander leaves before serving.

MARINATED MONKFISH WITH TOMATO COULIS

A LIGHT BUT WELL-FLAVOURED DISH, PERFECT FOR SUMMERTIME EATING AND ENJOYING AL FRESCO WITH A GLASS OR TWO OF CHILLED, FRUITY WINE, ROSÉ GOES WELL WITH THIS MEAL.

SERVES FOUR

INGREDIENTS
    30ml/2 tbsp olive oil
    finely grated rind and juice of 1 lime
    30ml/2 tbsp chopped fresh
       mixed herbs
    5ml/1 tsp Dijon mustard
    4 skinless, boneless monkfish fillets,
       about 175g/6oz each
    salt and ground black pepper
    fresh herb sprigs, to garnish
For the coulis
    4 plum tomatoes, peeled and chopped
    1 garlic clove, chopped
    15ml/1 tbsp olive oil
    15ml/1 tbsp tomato purée (paste)
    30ml/2 tbsp chopped fresh oregano
    5ml/1 tsp light soft brown sugar

COOK'S TIP
Monkfish may be hideous to look at, but the fish tastes wonderful, and is much sought after. Most of the flesh is to be found in the tail, which is the part that you will most often see at the fishmonger's. If you buy a whole tail, peel off the skin from the thick end towards the narrow section, then carefully pull off the pinkish membrane beneath. Fillet the fish by cutting through the flesh on either side of the backbone. This is very easy, as there are none of the usual side bones. The backbone can be used to make stock.

1 Place the oil, lime rind and juice, herbs, mustard and salt and pepper in a small bowl or jug and whisk together until thoroughly mixed.

2 Place the monkfish fillets in a shallow, non-metallic container and pour over the lime mixture. Turn the fish several times in the marinade to coat it. Cover and chill for 1–2 hours.

3 Meanwhile, make the coulis. Place all the coulis ingredients in a blender or food processor and process until smooth. Season to taste, then cover and chill until required.

4 Preheat the oven to 180°C/350°F/ Gas 4. Using a spatula, place each fillet on a sheet of greaseproof (waxed) paper big enough to hold it in a parcel.

5 Spoon a little marinade over each piece of fish. Gather the paper loosely over the fish and fold over the edges to secure the parcel tightly. Place on a baking sheet. Bake for 20–30 minutes until the fish fillets are cooked, tender and just beginning to flake.

6 Carefully unwrap the parcels and serve the fish fillets immediately, with a little of the chilled coulis served alongside, garnished with a few fresh herb sprigs.

VARIATION
The coulis can be served hot, if you prefer. Simply make as directed in the recipe and heat gently in a pan until almost boiling, before serving.

CHICKEN <u>AND</u> TOMATO CURRY

TENDER PIECES OF CHICKEN ARE LIGHTLY COOKED WITH FRESH VEGETABLES AND AROMATIC SPICES IN THIS DELICIOUS DISH. THE TOMATOES GO IN RIGHT AT THE END.

SERVES FOUR

INGREDIENTS
    675g/1½lb chicken breast portions
    30ml/2 tbsp oil
    2.5ml/½ tsp cumin seeds
    2.5ml/½ tsp fennel seeds
    1 onion, thickly sliced
    2 garlic cloves, crushed
    2.5cm/1in piece fresh root ginger,
      finely chopped
    15ml/1 tbsp curry paste
    225g/8oz broccoli, broken into florets
    12 tomatoes, cut into thick wedges
    5ml/1 tsp garam masala
    30ml/2 tbsp chopped fresh
      coriander (cilantro)
    naan bread, to serve

VARIATION
This works just as well with turkey breasts. Use thin turkey escalopes (scallops).

1 Pull the skin and any loose fat off the chicken breast portions. Use a knife to prise loose any remaining fat. Place each portion in turn between two sheets of clear film and pound with a meat mallet or pan to flatten evenly.

2 Using a sharp knife, cut the chicken fillets into cubes, each about the size of a walnut.

3 Heat the oil in a wok or large frying pan and fry the cumin and fennel seeds for 2 minutes until the seeds begin to splutter. Add the onion, garlic and ginger and cook for 5–7 minutes. Stir in the curry paste and cook for a further 2–3 minutes.

4 Add the broccoli florets and fry for about 5 minutes. Stir in the chicken cubes and fry for 5–8 minutes more.

5 Add the tomatoes, garam masala and chopped coriander. Cook for a further 5–10 minutes or until the chicken is tender. Serve with naan bread.

ENCHILADAS ^{WITH} HOT TOMATO ^{AND} GREEN CHILLI SAUCE

IN MEXICO, CHILLIES APPEAR IN ALMOST EVERY SAVOURY DISH, EITHER AS CHILLI POWDER OR CHOPPED, SLICED OR WHOLE. BY MEXICAN STANDARDS, THIS IS A MILD VERSION OF THE POPULAR CHICKEN ENCHILADAS. IF YOU LIKE YOUR FOOD HOT, ADD EXTRA CHILLIES TO THE TOMATO SAUCE.

SERVES FOUR

INGREDIENTS
    8 wheat tortillas
    175g/6oz Cheddar cheese, grated
    1 onion, finely chopped
    350g/12oz cooked chicken, cut into
      small chunks
    300ml/½ pint/1¼ cups sour cream
    1 avocado, sliced and tossed in
      lemon juice, to garnish
For the sauce
    1–2 fresh green chillies
    15ml/1 tbsp vegetable oil
    1 onion, chopped
    1 garlic clove, crushed
    400g/14oz can chopped tomatoes
    30ml/2 tbsp tomato purée (paste)
    salt and ground black pepper

1 To make the sauce, cut the chillies in half lengthways and carefully remove the cores and seeds. Slice the chillies very finely.

2 Heat the oil in a frying pan and fry the onion and garlic for about 3–4 minutes until softened. Stir in the tomatoes, tomato purée and chillies. Simmer gently, uncovered, for 12–15 minutes, stirring frequently.

3 Pour the sauce into a food processor or blender, and process until smooth. Return to the heat and cook very gently, uncovered, for a further 15 minutes. Season to taste, then set aside.

4 Preheat the oven to 180°C/350°F/ Gas 4. Butter a shallow ovenproof dish. Take one tortilla and sprinkle with some cheese and chopped onion, about 40g/1½oz of chicken and 15ml/1 tbsp of sauce. Pour over 15ml/1 tbsp of sour cream, roll up and place seam-side down in the dish.

5 Make 7 more enchiladas to fill the dish. Pour the remaining sauce over and sprinkle with the remaining cheese and onion. Bake for 25–30 minutes until the top is golden. Serve with the remaining sour cream, either poured over or in a separate container, and garnish with the sliced avocado.

SPANISH PORK <u>AND</u> SAUSAGE CASSEROLE

THIS DISH IS FROM THE CATALAN REGION OF SPAIN, AND COMBINES PORK CHOPS WITH SPICY BUTIFARRA SAUSAGES IN A RICH TOMATO SAUCE. YOU CAN FIND THESE SAUSAGES IN SOME SPANISH DELICATESSENS BUT, IF NOT, SWEET ITALIAN SAUSAGES WILL DO.

SERVES FOUR

INGREDIENTS
   30ml/2 tbsp olive oil
   4 boneless pork chops, about
      175g/6oz each
   4 *butifarra* or sweet Italian sausages
   1 onion, chopped
   2 garlic cloves, chopped
   120ml/4fl oz/½ cup dry white wine
   6 plum tomatoes, chopped
   1 bay leaf
   30ml/2 tbsp chopped fresh parsley
   salt and ground black pepper
   baked potatoes and green salad,
      to serve

1 Heat the oil in a large, deep frying pan. Cook the pork chops over a high heat until browned on both sides, then transfer to a plate.

2 Add the sausages, onion and garlic to the pan and cook over a medium heat until the sausages are browned and the onion softened, turning the sausages two or three times during cooking. Return the chops to the pan.

3 Stir in the wine, tomatoes, bay leaf and parsley. Season. Cover the pan and cook for 30 minutes.

4 Remove the sausages and cut into thick slices. Return them to the pan and heat through. Serve with baked potatoes and a green salad.

TORTILLA PIE WITH GREEN TOMATO SAUCE

THIS IS A POPULAR MEXICAN BREAKFAST DISH, KNOWN AS CHILAQUILES. THE FRIED TORTILLA STRIPS STAY CRISP IN THE TOMATO, CREAM AND CHEESE TOPPING.

SERVES SIX

INGREDIENTS

    30ml/2 tbsp vegetable oil
    500g/1¼lb minced (ground) pork
    3 garlic cloves, crushed
    10ml/2 tsp dried oregano
    5ml/1 tsp ground cinnamon
    2.5ml/½ tsp ground cloves
    2.5ml/½ tsp ground black pepper
    30ml/2 tbsp dry sherry
    5ml/1 tsp caster (superfine) sugar
    5ml/1 tsp salt
    12 corn tortillas
    oil, for frying
    350g/12oz/3 cups grated Monterey
      Jack or mild Cheddar cheese
    300ml/½ pint/1¼ cups crème fraîche
For the green tomato sauce
    300g/11oz/scant 2 cups canned
      green tomatoes, drained
    60ml/4 tbsp stock or water
    2 fresh chillies, seeded and chopped
    2 garlic cloves
    small bunch of fresh coriander
      (cilantro)
    120ml/4fl oz/½ cup sour cream

1 Preheat the oven to 180°C/350°F/ Gas 4. Heat the fat in a large pan. Add the minced pork and crushed garlic. Stir over a medium heat until the meat has browned, then stir in the oregano, cinnamon, cloves and pepper.

2 Cook for 3–4 minutes more, stirring constantly, then add the sherry, sugar and salt. Stir for 3–4 minutes until all the flavours are blended, then remove the pan from the heat.

3 Cut the tortillas into 2cm/¾in strips. Pour oil into a frying pan to a depth of 2cm/¾in and heat to 190°C/375°F. Fry the tortilla strips in batches until crisp and golden brown all over.

4 Spread half the minced pork mixture in an ovenproof dish. Top with half the tortilla strips and grated cheese, then add dollops of crème fraîche. Repeat the layers. Bake for 20–25 minutes, or until bubbling.

5 To make the sauce, put all the ingredients except the sour cream in a food processor or blender (and reserve a little coriander for sprinkling). Process until smooth. Scrape into a pan, bring to the boil, then lower the heat and simmer for 5 minutes.

6 Stir the sour cream into the sauce, with salt and pepper to taste. Pour the mixture over the dish and serve immediately, sprinkled with coriander.

POLPETTES <u>WITH</u> MOZZARELLA <u>AND</u> TOMATO

These Italian meatballs are made with beef and topped with mozzarella cheese and tomato. They taste as good as they look.

SERVES SIX

INGREDIENTS
½ slice white bread, crusts removed
45ml/3 tbsp milk
675g/1½lb minced (ground) beef
1 egg, beaten
50g/2oz/⅔ cup dry breadcrumbs
vegetable oil, for frying
2 beefsteak or other large tomatoes,
    sliced to make 6 slices
15ml/1 tbsp chopped fresh oregano
6 slices mozzarella cheese
6 canned anchovies, drained and
    halved lengthways
salt and ground black pepper

1 Preheat the oven to 200°C/400°F/ Gas 6. Put the bread and milk into a small pan and heat very gently, until the bread absorbs all the milk. Transfer the mixture to a small bowl, mash it to a pulp and leave to cool.

2 Put the beef into a bowl with the bread mixture and the egg, and season with salt and pepper. Mix well, then shape the mixture into 6 patties. Sprinkle the breadcrumbs on to a plate and press the patties with the crumbs until they are thoroughly coated.

3 Heat oil to a depth of about 5mm/¼in in a large frying pan. Add the patties and fry for 2 minutes on each side, until brown. Transfer to a greased ovenproof dish, in a single layer.

4 Lay a slice of tomato on top of each patty, sprinkle with the oregano and season with salt and pepper. Place the mozzarella slices on top. Arrange two strips of anchovy, placed in a cross, on top of each slice of mozzarella. Bake for 10–15 minutes, until the mozzarella has melted. Serve the polpettes hot, straight from the oven.

VARIATION
Use strips of sun-dried tomato on the polpettes instead of anchovies.

ALBONDIGAS ^{WITH} SPICY TOMATO SAUCE

THESE TASTY MEXICAN MEATBALLS ARE ABSOLUTELY DELICIOUS, AND THE DRIED CHIPOTLE CHILLI GIVES THE TOMATO SAUCE A DISTINCTIVE, SLIGHTLY SMOKY FLAVOUR.

SERVES FOUR

INGREDIENTS
225g/8oz minced (ground) pork
225g/8oz lean minced (ground) beef
1 medium onion, finely chopped
50g/2oz/1 cup fresh
  white breadcrumbs
5ml/1 tsp dried oregano
2.5ml/½ tsp ground cumin
2.5ml/½ tsp salt
2.5ml/½ tsp ground black pepper
1 egg, beaten
oil, for frying
fresh oregano sprigs, to garnish
For the sauce
1 chipotle chilli, seeded
15ml/1 tbsp vegetable oil
1 onion, finely chopped
2 garlic cloves, crushed
175ml/6fl oz/¾ cup beef stock
400g/14oz can chopped tomatoes
105ml/7 tbsp passata (bottled
  strained tomatoes)

COOK'S TIP
Dampen your hands before shaping the meatballs so the mixture will be less likely to stick.

1 Mix the minced pork and beef in a bowl. Add the onion, breadcrumbs, oregano, cumin, salt and pepper. Mix with clean hands until all the ingredients are well combined.

2 Mix the egg in well, then roll the mixture into 4cm/1½in balls. Put these on a baking sheet and chill while you prepare the sauce.

3 Cover the dried chilli with hot water and soak for 15 minutes. Heat the oil in a pan and fry the onion and garlic for 3–4 minutes until softened.

4 Drain the chilli, reserving the soaking water, then chop it and add it to the onion mixture. Fry for 1 minute, then stir in the beef stock, tomatoes, passata and soaking water, with salt and pepper to taste. Bring to the boil, lower the heat and simmer, stirring occasionally, while you cook the meatballs.

5 Heat the oil for frying in a flameproof casserole and fry the meatballs in batches for about 5 minutes, turning them occasionally, until they have browned all over. Drain off the oil and return all the meatballs to the casserole.

6 Pour the tomato and chilli sauce over the meatballs and simmer on a hotplate (burner) for about 10 minutes, occasionally stirring gently so that the meatballs are coated. Be careful that they do not disintegrate with stirring. Garnish the dish with the oregano and serve.

PROVENÇAL BEEF AND OLIVE DAUBE

A DAUBE IS A FRENCH METHOD OF BRAISING MEAT WITH WINE AND HERBS. THIS VERSION FROM THE NICE AREA IN THE SOUTH OF FRANCE ALSO INCLUDES BLACK OLIVES AND TOMATOES.

SERVES SIX

INGREDIENTS
    1.3–1.6kg/3–3½lb topside (pot roast)
        of beef
    225g/8oz lardons, or thick
        streaky (fatty) bacon cut
        into strips
    225g/8oz carrots, sliced thickly
    1 bay leaf
    1 fresh thyme sprig
    2 fresh parsley stalks
    3 garlic cloves
    225g/8oz/2 cups pitted
        black olives
    400g/14oz can chopped tomatoes, or
        if not available, a can of whole
        tomatoes, chopped
    crusty bread, flageolet (small
        cannellini) beans or pasta, to serve
For the marinade
    120ml/4fl oz/½ cup extra
        virgin olive oil or other
        mild oil
    1 onion, sliced
    4 shallots, sliced
    1 celery stick, sliced
    1 carrot, sliced
    150ml/¼ pint/⅔ cup red wine
    6 whole black peppercorns
    2 garlic cloves, sliced
    1 bay leaf
    1 fresh thyme sprig
    2 fresh parsley stalks
    salt and ground black pepper

VARIATIONS
• This dish can be varied quite easily, simply keep the main ingredients the same and change the herbs: instead of thyme and parsley, try rosemary.
• If you prefer, use chicken instead of beef and make the marinade with white wine.
• You could vary this dish further by choosing sweet white wine or adding some extra sugar, and leaving out the olives and herbs in favour of Chinese five-spice powder. This will give the dish a more oriental flavour.

1 To make the marinade, gently heat the oil in a large, shallow pan. Do not let it become too hot or it will smoke. Add the sliced onion, shallots, celery and carrot, then cook for 2 minutes.

2 Lower the heat and wait until the ingredients have cooled slightly, then add the red wine, peppercorns, garlic, bay leaf, thyme and parsley stalks.

3 Season with salt, then cover and leave to simmer on a gentle heat for 15–20 minutes, stirring occasionally. Set the pan aside.

4 Place the beef in a large glass or earthenware dish and pour over the cooled marinade from the frying pan.

5 Cover the dish with a cloth or greaseproof (waxed) paper and let the beef marinate in a cool place or in the fridge for 12 hours. Turn the meat every few hours if possible, but at least once during this time.

6 Preheat the oven to 160°C/325°F/ Gas 3. Lift the meat out of the marinade and fit snugly into a casserole. Add the lardons or bacon and carrots, along with the herbs and garlic.

7 Strain in all the marinade. Cover the casserole with greaseproof paper, then the lid and cook in the oven for 2½ hours.

8 Remove the casserole from the oven, blot the surface of the liquid with kitchen paper to remove the surplus fat, or use a spoon to skim it off, then stir in the olives and tomatoes.

9 Recover the casserole, return to the oven and cook for a further 30 minutes. Carve the meat into thick slices and serve it with chunky crusty bread, plain boiled flageolet beans or pasta.

COOK'S TIP
For those with an alcohol sensitivity, red grape juice and a squeeze of lemon or lime juice can be substituted for the red wine.

LAMB GOULASH WITH TOMATOES AND PEPPERS

GOULASH IS A POPULAR AND TRADITIONAL DISH THAT HAS TRAVELLED ACROSS THE WORLD FROM HUNGARY — THIS RECIPE HAS A WONDERFUL COMBINATION OF TOMATOES, PAPRIKA, GREEN PEPPERS, MARJORAM AND A HINT OF FRESH GARLIC.

SERVES FOUR TO SIX

INGREDIENTS

30ml/2 tbsp vegetable oil
900g/2lb lean lamb, trimmed and cut
  into cubes
1 large onion, roughly chopped
2 garlic cloves, crushed
3 green (bell) peppers, seeded
  and diced
30ml/2 tbsp paprika
2 x 400g/14oz cans chopped tomatoes
15ml/1 tbsp chopped fresh flat
  leaf parsley
5ml/1 tsp chopped fresh marjoram
30ml/2 tbsp plain (all-purpose) flour
salt and ground black pepper
green salad, to serve

COOK'S TIPS
• Lard (shortening) is traditionally used for frying the lamb cubes, and can be substituted for the vegetable oil.
• When frying the lamb cubes, it is important not to overload the pan. Cook them in batches if necessary.
• Sour cream is delicious with goulash. Offer a bowl at the table.

1 Heat the oil in a frying pan. Fry the pieces of lamb for 5–8 minutes, stirring frequently with a wooden spoon, or until browned on all sides. Season well.

2 Stir in the chopped onion and crushed garlic, and cook for a further 2 minutes. Add the diced green peppers, then sprinkle over the paprika and stir it in.

3 Pour in the tomatoes and enough water, if needed, to cover the meat in the pan. Stir in the herbs. Bring to the boil, reduce the heat, cover and simmer very gently for 1½ hours or until the lamb is tender.

4 Blend the flour with 60ml/4 tbsp water and pour into the stew. Bring back to the boil, then reduce the heat to a simmer and cook, stirring occasionally, until thickened. Serve with a crisp green salad.

ROMANIAN KEBABS

KEBABS ARE POPULAR WORLDWIDE, LARGELY BECAUSE THEY ARE SO EASILY ADAPTED TO SUIT EVERYONE'S TASTE. IN THIS RECIPE, LEAN LAMB IS MARINATED, THEN COOKED WITH CHUNKS OF VEGETABLES TO PRODUCE A DELICIOUS, COLOURFUL AND HEALTHY MEAL.

SERVES SIX

INGREDIENTS

675g/1½lb lean lamb, cut into
    4cm/1½in cubes
12 button (pearl) onions
2 green (bell) peppers, seeded and
    cut into 12 pieces
12 cherry tomatoes
12 button (pearl) mushrooms
lemon slices and rosemary sprigs,
    to garnish
freshly cooked rice and crusty bread,
    to serve
For the marinade
    juice of 1 lemon
    120ml/4fl oz/½ cup red wine
    1 onion, finely chopped
    60ml/4 tbsp olive oil
    2.5ml/½ tsp dried sage
    2.5ml/½ tsp chopped fresh rosemary
    salt and ground black pepper

VARIATIONS
• Use rump (round) steak instead of lamb. Cut it into strips, marinate it as suggested, then interleave the strips on the skewers, with the onions, cherry tomatoes and mushrooms. Omit the green peppers.
• These kebabs are just as delicious cooked on a barbecue (grill).

1 For the marinade, combine the lemon juice, red wine, onion, olive oil, herbs and seasoning in a bowl. Stir the cubes of lamb into the marinade. Cover and chill in the refrigerator for 2–12 hours, stirring occasionally.

2 Remove the lamb pieces from the marinade and thread on 6 skewers with the onions, peppers, tomatoes and mushrooms. Preheat the grill (broiler).

3 Brush the kebabs with marinade and grill (broil) for 10–15 minutes, turning once. Arrange on cooked rice, with lemon and rosemary. Serve with crusty bread.

An essential ingredient in so many vegetarian dishes, tomatoes are often used as the basis for sauces — try Mediterranean Rolls with Tomato Sauce or Rigatoni with Tomatoes and Fresh Herbs. They play an important role in one-pot dishes, such as the warming Bean and Tomato Casserole, and Tomato, Pistachio and Sesame Pilau, but it is in treats like Onions Stuffed with Goat's Cheese and Sun-dried Tomatoes, and Classic Margherita Pizza that they really take centre stage.

Vegetarian
Main Meals

RIGATONI WITH TOMATOES AND FRESH HERBS

THIS PRETTY-COLOURED PASTA DISH RELIES FOR ITS SUCCESS ON THE BEST ITALIAN CANNED TOMATOES AND TENDER YOUNG HERBS, FRESHLY PICKED. FOR A REAL GOURMET TREAT, USE FRESH TOMATOES, SKINNED AND PURÉED. ADD A LITTLE SUGAR IF THE TOMATOES ARE NOT AT THE PEAK OF RIPENESS.

SERVES SIX TO EIGHT

INGREDIENTS

1 onion
1 carrot
1 celery stick
60ml/4 tbsp olive oil
1 garlic clove, thinly sliced
a few leaves each of fresh basil,
   thyme and oregano or marjoram
2 x 400g/14oz cans chopped Italian
   plum tomatoes
15ml/1 tbsp sun-dried tomato paste
5ml/1 tsp granulated sugar
about 90ml/6 tbsp dry red or white
   wine (optional)
350g/12oz/3 cups dried rigatoni
salt and ground black pepper
coarsely shaved Parmesan cheese,
   to serve

COOK'S TIP
Large pasta tubes are best for this recipe, as they capture the wonderful tomato and herb sauce. If you can't get rigatoni, try penne or penne rigate (ridged penne).

1 Chop the onion, carrot and celery stick finely, either in a food processor or by hand, with a sharp knife.

2 Heat the olive oil in a medium pan, add the garlic slices and stir over a very low heat for 1–2 minutes. Do not let the garlic burn.

3 Add the chopped vegetables and the fresh herbs, reserving a few to garnish. Cook over a low heat, stirring frequently, for 5–7 minutes until the vegetables have softened and are lightly coloured.

4 Add the canned tomatoes, tomato paste and sugar, then stir in the wine, if using. Add salt and pepper to taste. Bring to the boil, stirring, then lower the heat to a gentle simmer. Cook, stirring often, for about 45 minutes.

5 Cook the pasta in lightly salted boiling water for 10–12 minutes, drain and tip into a warmed bowl. Pour the sauce over the pasta and toss well. Garnish with the reserved herbs. Serve immediately, with shavings of Parmesan handed separately.

SPAGHETTI <u>WITH</u> FRESH TOMATO SAUCE

THE HEAT FROM THE PASTA WILL RELEASE THE DELICIOUS FLAVOURS OF THIS SAUCE. ONLY USE THE TRULY RED AND SOFT PLUM TOMATOES, AS THE AROMATIC QUALITY OF REALLY GOOD TOMATOES IMPROVES THE FLAVOUR OF THIS SAUCE — LARGE RIPE BEEFSTEAK TOMATOES ARE ALSO IDEAL.

SERVES FOUR

INGREDIENTS

675g/1½lb ripe Italian
  plum tomatoes or sweet
  cherry tomatoes
60ml/4 tbsp extra virgin olive oil or
  sunflower oil
1 onion, finely chopped
350g/12oz fresh or dried spaghetti
a small handful fresh basil leaves
salt and ground black pepper
coarsely shaved Parmesan cheese,
  to serve

COOK'S TIPS

• The Italian plum tomatoes called San Marzano are the best variety to use. When fully ripe, they have thin skins that peel off easily.
• In Italy, cooks often make this sauce in bulk in the summer months and freeze it for later use. Let it cool, then freeze in usable quantities in rigid containers. Thaw before reheating.

1 With a sharp knife, cut a cross in the base end of each tomato. Plunge the tomatoes, a few at a time, into a bowl of boiling water. Leave for 30 seconds or so, then lift them out with a slotted spoon and drop them into a bowl of cold water. Drain well. The skin will have begun to peel back from the crosses. Remove it entirely.

2 Place the tomatoes on a chopping board and cut into quarters, then eighths, and chop as finely as possible

3 Heat the oil in a large pan, add the onion and cook over a low heat, stirring frequently, for about 5 minutes until softened and lightly coloured.

4 Add the tomatoes, season with salt and pepper to taste, bring to a simmer, then turn the heat down to low and cover the pan with a lid. Cook, stirring occasionally, for 30–40 minutes until the mixture is thick.

5 Meanwhile, cook the pasta according to the instructions on the packet. Shred the basil leaves finely, or tear them into small pieces.

6 Remove the sauce from the heat, stir in the basil and taste for seasoning again. Drain the pasta into a colander. Tip the spaghetti into a warmed bowl, pour the sauce over and toss the mixture well. Serve immediately, with shaved Parmesan handed around in a separate bowl.

INDIAN RICE ^{WITH} TOMATOES ^{AND} SPINACH

THIS TASTY RICE DISH IS AN AROMATIC, RATHER THAN HOT INDIAN DISH. PERFECT FOR THOSE WITH DELICATE PALATES. IT CAN BE SERVED BY ITSELF OR AS ONE OF A NUMBER OF SMALLER DISHES.

SERVES FOUR

INGREDIENTS

    30ml/2 tbsp sunflower oil
    15g/½oz/1 tbsp ghee or butter
    1 onion, chopped
    2 garlic cloves, crushed
    5 tomatoes, peeled, seeded
      and chopped
    225g/8oz/generous 1 cup brown
      basmati rice, soaked
    10ml/2 tsp *dhana jeera* powder or
      5ml/1 tsp ground coriander and
      5ml/1 tsp ground cumin
    2 carrots, coarsely grated
    900ml/1½ pints/3¾ cups vegetable
      stock
    275g/10oz baby spinach
      leaves, washed
    115g/4oz/1 cup unsalted cashew
      nuts, toasted
    salt and ground black pepper

1 Heat the oil and ghee or butter in a flameproof casserole and fry the onion and garlic for 5 minutes. Add the chopped tomatoes and cook, stirring, until slightly thickened.

2 Drain the rice, add it to the casserole and cook gently for 1–2 minutes, stirring, until the rice is coated with the tomato and onion mixture.

3 Stir in the *dhana jeera* powder or the ground coriander and cumin, then add the grated carrots and season. Pour in the stock and mix well.

4 Bring to the boil, then cover tightly and simmer over a very low heat for 20–25 minutes until the rice is tender. Lay the baby spinach leaves on the surface of the rice, cover again and cook for 2–3 minutes until the spinach has wilted.

5 Fold the spinach into the rest of the rice and check the seasoning. Sprinkle with the toasted cashew nuts and serve in warmed bowls.

COOK'S TIP
If you can't get baby spinach leaves, use larger fresh spinach leaves. Remove any tough stalks and chop the leaves roughly. A sweeter and less acidic alternative is to use Swiss chard – again, the stalks will need to be removed before use.

PROVENÇAL RICE

ONE OF THE GLORIOUS THINGS ABOUT FOOD FROM THE SOUTH OF FRANCE IS ITS COLOUR — SWEET CHERRY TOMATOES, PURPLE AUBERGINES AND TENDER GREEN COURGETTES ARE A DELICIOUS COMBINATION.

SERVES FOUR

INGREDIENTS

2 onions
90ml/6 tbsp extra virgin olive oil or sunflower oil
225g/8oz/generous 1 cup long grain brown rice
10ml/2 tsp mustard seeds
600ml/1 pint/2½ cups vegetable stock
1 large or 2 small red (bell) peppers, seeded and cut into chunks
1 small aubergine (eggplant), cubed
2–3 courgettes (zucchini), sliced
about 12 cherry tomatoes
5–6 fresh basil leaves, torn into pieces
2 garlic cloves, finely chopped
60ml/4 tbsp white wine
60ml/4 tbsp passata (bottled strained tomatoes) or tomato juice
2 hard-boiled (hard-cooked) eggs, cut into wedges
8 stuffed green olives, sliced
15ml/1 tbsp capers
3 sun-dried tomatoes in oil, drained and sliced (optional)
sea salt and ground pepper

1 Preheat the oven to 200°C/400°F/Gas 6. Roughly chop 1 onion. Heat 30ml/2 tbsp of the oil in a pan and fry the chopped onion over a low heat for 5–6 minutes until softened.

2 Add the rice and mustard seeds. Cook, stirring, for 2 minutes, then add the stock and a little salt. Bring to the boil, then lower the heat, cover and simmer for 35 minutes until the rice is tender and fairly dry.

3 Meanwhile, cut the remaining onion into wedges. Put these in a roasting pan with the peppers, aubergine, courgettes and cherry tomatoes. Sprinkle over the torn basil leaves and chopped garlic. Pour over the remaining olive oil and sprinkle with sea salt and black pepper. Roast for 15–20 minutes until the vegetables begin to char, stirring halfway through cooking. Remove from the oven, then reduce the temperature to 180°C/350°F/Gas 4.

4 Spoon the rice into an earthenware casserole. Put the roasted vegetables on top, together with any juices from the roasting pan, then pour over the combined wine and passata or tomato juice.

5 Arrange the egg wedges on top of the vegetables, with the sliced olives, capers and sun-dried tomatoes, if using. Dot with butter, cover and cook for 15–20 minutes until heated through. Serve immediately, in warmed bowls.

TOMATO, PISTACHIO AND SESAME PILAU

FOR A SIMPLE YET REALLY TASTY DISH, YOU CAN'T GO WRONG WITH THIS NUTTY PILAU — THE CARDAMOM SEEDS GIVE IT A REALLY EXOTIC FLAVOUR.

SERVES FOUR

INGREDIENTS
- 12 fresh plum or round tomatoes
- 1 red (bell) pepper
- 225g/8oz/1⅓ cups brown basmati rice
- pinch of saffron threads
- 600ml/1 pint/2½ cups vegetable stock or half white wine and half water
- pinch of salt
- 4–5 cardamom pods
- 50g/2oz/½ cup pistachio nuts, shelled and roughly chopped, toasted if you like
- 30ml/2 tbsp sesame seeds or sunflower seeds, toasted

1 Plunge the tomatoes into boiling water for 30 seconds, then refresh in cold water. Peel off the skins and chop the tomatoes.

2 Halve the pepper and remove the seeds. Turn so that the cut side of the pepper is flat on the chopping board and cut into chunks.

3 Wash the rice in several changes of cold water, then drain and tip into a bowl. Pour over fresh cold water to cover and soak for 30 minutes.

4 Meanwhile, soak the saffron threads in the vegetable stock, or the wine and water mixture.

5 Drain the rice, then tip it into a pan. Add the saffron liquid and bring to the boil. Lower the heat, cover and simmer for 25 minutes. Meanwhile, break open the cardamom pods, extract the seeds and crush them finely.

6 Stir the tomato, peppers and crushed seeds into the rice mixture. Cook for a further 5–10 minutes until the rice is tender and all the liquid has been absorbed. If the liquid is absorbed before the rice is cooked, add a little more. It should not be necessary to drain the rice.

7 Tip the rice into a serving dish and sprinkle the pistachio nuts and sesame or sunflower seeds over the top.

RED FRIED RICE

THIS VIBRANT RICE DISH OWES AS MUCH OF ITS APPEAL TO THE BRIGHT COLOURS OF RED ONION, RED PEPPER AND CHERRY TOMATOES AS IT DOES TO THEIR DISTINCTIVE FLAVOURS.

SERVES TWO

INGREDIENTS

115g/4oz basmati rice
30ml/2 tbsp groundnut (peanut) oil
1 small red onion, chopped
1 red (bell) pepper, seeded and chopped
225g/8oz cherry tomatoes, halved
2 eggs, beaten
salt and ground black pepper
parsley, chopped, to garnish

VARIATION
For a nuttier flavour, substitute brown basmati rice. It will take a little longer to cook – about 25–30 minutes.

1 Wash the rice several times under cold running water. Drain well. Bring a large pan of salted water to the boil, add the rice and cook for 10–12 minutes until tender.

2 Meanwhile, heat the oil in a wok until very hot. Add the onion and red pepper and stir-fry for 2–3 minutes. Add the cherry tomatoes and stir-fry for a further 2 minutes.

3 Break the eggs into a bowl and beat with a fork or a whisk until the texture becomes uniform.

4 Add the eggs to the wok all at once. Cook for 30 seconds without stirring, then stir to break up the eggs as they set.

5 Drain the cooked rice thoroughly, ensuring that no water remains. Add it to the wok and toss it over the heat to combine with the vegetable and egg mixture for 3 minutes. Season with salt and pepper. Sprinkle over the parsley, to garnish.

TOMATO <u>AND</u> BLACK OLIVE TART

THIS DELICIOUS TART HAS A FRESH, RICH MEDITERRANEAN FLAVOUR. SINCE THE FLAVOUR OF THE TOMATOES IS QUITE OBVIOUS IN THIS DISH, IT IS PERFECT FOR TRYING DIFFERENT TOMATO VARIETIES.

SERVES FOUR

INGREDIENTS
   6 firm plum tomatoes, or other tasty
      tomatoes
   75g/3oz ripe Brie cheese
   about 16 black olives, pitted
   3 eggs, beaten
   300ml/½ pint/1¼ cups milk
   30ml/2 tbsp chopped fresh herbs,
      such as parsley, marjoram or basil
   salt and ground black pepper
   salad or cooked vegetables, to serve
For the pastry
   115g/4oz/½ cup butter
   225g/8oz/2 cups plain (all-purpose)
      flour, plus extra for dusting
   1 egg yolk

1 To make the pastry, rub together the butter and flour until it resembles fine breadcrumbs. Blend in the egg yolk and a little cold water, then mix thoroughly to form a smooth dough. Cover and leave for 10 minutes.

2 Preheat the oven to 190°C/375°F/ Gas 5. Roll out the pastry thinly on a lightly floured surface. Line a 28 x 18cm/ 11 x 7in loose-based rectangular flan tin (tart pan), trimming off any overhanging edges with a sharp knife.

3 Line the pastry case with greaseproof (waxed) paper and weigh it down with baking beans, and bake blind for 15 minutes. Remove the paper and beans, and bake for a further 5 minutes until the base is crisp.

4 Meanwhile, slice the tomatoes, cube the cheese, and slice the olives. Mix together the eggs, milk, seasoning and herbs.

5 Place the prepared flan case on a baking tray, arrange the tomatoes, cheese and olives on the base, then pour in the egg mixture.

6 Transfer carefully to the oven and bake for about 40 minutes until just firm and turning golden. Slice hot or cool in the tin and then serve with salad or cooked vegetables.

CLASSIC MARGHERITA PIZZA

THIS TOMATO, BASIL AND MOZZARELLA PIZZA IS SIMPLE TO PREPARE. THE SWEET FLAVOUR OF SUN-RIPE TOMATOES WORKS WONDERFULLY WITH THE BASIL AND MOZZARELLA.

SERVES TWO

INGREDIENTS
  30ml/2 tbsp olive oil
  1 onion, finely chopped
  1 garlic clove, crushed
  400g/14oz can chopped tomatoes
  15ml/1 tbsp tomato purée (paste)
  pinch of granulated sugar
  15ml/1 tbsp chopped fresh basil
  150g/5oz mozzarella cheese
  4 ripe tomatoes, sliced
  6–8 fresh basil leaves
  30ml/2 tbsp grated Parmesan cheese
  salt and ground black pepper
For the pizza base
  225g/8oz/2 cups strong white
    (bread) flour
  5ml/1 tsp salt
  2.5ml/½ tsp easy-blend (rapid-rise)
    dried yeast
  15ml/1 tbsp olive oil
  150ml/¼ pint/⅔ cup warm water

1 Make the pizza base. Place the dry ingredients in a bowl. Add the oil and water. Mix to a soft dough and knead for 10 minutes. Cover and put in a warm place until doubled in bulk.

2 Preheat the oven to 220°C/425°F/ Gas 7. Make the topping. Fry the onion and garlic for 5 minutes in half the oil. Stir in the tomatoes, purée and sugar. Cook for 5 minutes. Stir in the basil and seasoning.

3 Knead the dough lightly for 5 minutes, then roll out to a round and place on a baking sheet.

4 Use a spoon to spread the tomato topping evenly over the base. Cut the mozzarella cheese and fresh tomatoes into thick slices. Arrange them in a circle, alternating the cheese with the tomato slices.

5 Roughly tear the basil leaves, add to the pizza and sprinkle with the Parmesan cheese. Drizzle over the remaining oil and season well with black pepper. Bake for 15–20 minutes until crisp and golden. Serve immediately.

ONIONS STUFFED <u>WITH</u> GOAT'S CHEESE <u>AND</u> SUN-DRIED TOMATOES

ROASTED ONIONS AND GOAT'S CHEESE ARE A WINNING COMBINATION. THESE STUFFED ONIONS MAKE AN EXCELLENT MAIN COURSE WHEN SERVED WITH A RICE OR CRACKED WHEAT PILAFF.

SERVES FOUR

INGREDIENTS

4 large onions
150g/5oz goat's cheese, crumbled
  or cubed
50g/2oz/1 cup fresh breadcrumbs
8 sun-dried tomatoes in olive oil,
  drained and chopped
1–2 garlic cloves, finely chopped
2.5ml/½ tsp chopped fresh
  thyme leaves
30ml/2 tbsp chopped fresh parsley
1 small egg, beaten
45ml/3 tbsp pine nuts, toasted
30ml/2 tbsp olive oil (from the jar of
  sun-dried tomatoes)
salt and ground black pepper

1 Bring a large pan of lightly salted water to the boil. Add the whole onions in their skins and boil for 10 minutes. Drain and cool, then cut each onion in half horizontally and slip off the skins, keeping the onion halves intact.

2 Using a teaspoon to scoop out the flesh, remove the centre of each onion, leaving a thick shell. Reserve the flesh on a board and place the shells in an oiled ovenproof dish. Preheat the oven to 190°C/375°F/Gas 5.

3 Chop the scooped-out onion flesh and place it in a bowl. Add the goat's cheese, breadcrumbs, sun-dried tomatoes, garlic, thyme, half the parsley and egg. Mix well, then season to taste with salt and pepper, and add the toasted pine nuts.

4 Divide the stuffing among the onions and cover with foil. Bake for about 25 minutes. Uncover, drizzle with the oil and cook for another 30–40 minutes, until the filling is bubbling and the onions are well cooked. Baste occasionally during cooking. When cooked, sprinkle with the remaining parsley to garnish.

VARIATIONS
• Omit the goat's cheese and add 115g/4oz finely chopped mushrooms and 1 grated carrot.
• Substitute feta cheese for the goat's cheese and raisins for the pine nuts.
• Substitute smoked mozzarella for the goat's cheese and substitute pistachio nuts for the pine nuts.
• Use red and yellow (bell) peppers preserved in olive oil instead of sun-dried tomatoes.

MEDITERRANEAN ROLLS WITH TOMATO SAUCE

THESE LITTLE ROLLS OF AUBERGINE WRAPPED AROUND A FILLING OF RICOTTA AND RICE MAKE AN INSPIRED ADDITION TO A SUMMER BUFFET TABLE OR A GREEK OR TURKISH-STYLE MEZE.

SERVES FOUR

INGREDIENTS

    2 aubergines (eggplant)
    olive oil, or sunflower oil for
      shallow frying
    75g/3oz/scant ½ cup ricotta cheese
    75g/3oz/scant ½ cup soft goat's
      cheese
    225g/8oz/2 cups cooked long grain
      white rice
    15ml/1 tbsp chopped fresh basil
    5ml/1 tsp chopped fresh mint, plus
      mint sprigs, to garnish
    salt and ground black pepper
For the tomato sauce
    15ml/1 tbsp olive oil
    1 red onion, finely chopped
    1 garlic clove, crushed
    400g/14oz can chopped tomatoes
    120ml/4fl oz/½ cup vegetable stock
      or white wine or a mixture
    15ml/1 tbsp chopped fresh parsley

COOK'S TIP
Cut each aubergine into 4–5 slices, discarding the two outer slices, which consist largely of skin. If you prefer to use less oil for the aubergines, brush each slice with just a little oil, then grill (broil) until evenly browned.

1 Make the tomato sauce. Heat the oil in a small pan and fry the onion and garlic for 3–4 minutes until softened. Add the tomatoes, vegetable stock and/or wine, and parsley. Season well. Bring to the boil, then lower the heat and simmer for 10–12 minutes until slightly thickened, stirring.

2 Preheat the oven to 190°C/375°F/ Gas 5. Slice the aubergines lengthways. Heat the oil in a large frying pan and fry the aubergine slices until they are golden brown on both sides. Drain on kitchen paper. Mix the ricotta, goat's cheese, rice, basil and mint in a bowl. Season well with salt and pepper.

3 Place a generous spoonful of the cheese and rice mixture at one end of each aubergine slice and roll up. Arrange the rolls side by side in a shallow ovenproof dish. Pour the tomato sauce over the top and bake for 10–15 minutes until heated through. Garnish with the mint sprigs and serve.

VEGETABLE MOUSSAKA

THIS IS A REALLY FLAVOURSOME VEGETARIAN ALTERNATIVE TO CLASSIC MEAT MOUSSAKA. SERVE IT WITH WARM BREAD AND A GLASS OR TWO OF RUSTIC RED WINE.

SERVES SIX

INGREDIENTS
    450g/1lb aubergines (eggplant),
      sliced
    115g/4oz/½ cup whole green lentils
    600ml/1 pint/2½ cups vegetable stock
    1 bay leaf
    225g/8oz fresh tomatoes
    45ml/3 tbsp olive oil
    1 onion, sliced
    1 garlic clove, crushed
    225g/8oz/3 cups mushrooms, sliced
    400g/14oz can chickpeas, rinsed
      and drained
    400g/14oz can chopped tomatoes
    30ml/2 tbsp tomato purée (paste)
    10ml/2 tsp dried basil
    300ml/½ pint/1¼ cups natural
      (plain) yogurt
    3 eggs
    50g/2oz/½ cup grated mature (sharp)
      Cheddar cheese
    salt and ground black pepper
    fresh flat leaf parsley sprigs,
      to garnish

VARIATION

You can make various creamy toppings for this moussaka by substituting cream or white sauce for the yogurt. Or, if you are short of time, you could consider using a packet sauce – anything from parsley sauce to béchamel sauce works excellently with this recipe.

1 Sprinkle the aubergine slices with salt and place in a colander. Cover and leave for 30 minutes to allow any bitter juices to be extracted.

2 Meanwhile, place the lentils, stock and bay leaf in a pan. Cover, bring to the boil and simmer for about 20 minutes until the lentils are just tender. Drain well and keep warm.

3 If wished skin the fresh tomatoes then cut them into pieces.

4 Heat 15ml/1 tbsp of the oil in a large pan, add the onion and garlic, and cook for 5 minutes, stirring. Stir in the lentils, mushrooms, chickpeas, fresh and canned tomatoes, tomato purée, basil and 45ml/3 tbsp water. Bring to the boil, cover and simmer gently for 10 minutes.

5 Preheat the oven to 180°C/350°F/ Gas 4. Rinse the aubergine slices, drain and pat dry. Heat the remaining oil in a frying pan and fry the slices in batches for 3–4 minutes, turning once.

6 Season the lentil mixture. Layer the aubergines and lentils in an ovenproof dish, starting with aubergines and finishing with the lentil mixture.

7 Beat together the yogurt, eggs and salt and pepper, and pour the mixture into the dish. Sprinkle the cheese on top and bake for 45 minutes. Serve, garnished with flat leaf parsley sprigs.

BEAN <u>AND</u> TOMATO CASSEROLE

JUICY TOMATOES AND FILLING CANNELLINI BEANS BAKED — A GREAT DISH FOR A COLD DAY.

SERVES FOUR

INGREDIENTS
45ml/3 tbsp extra virgin olive oil or
   sunflower oil
45ml/3 tbsp chopped fresh flat
   leaf parsley
400g/14oz can cannellini beans,
   rinsed and drained
1kg/2¼lb firm ripe tomatoes
5ml/1 tsp caster (superfine) sugar
40g/1½oz/scant 1 cup
   day-old breadcrumbs
2.5ml/½ tsp chilli powder or paprika
salt
chopped fresh parsley, to garnish
rye bread, to serve

1 Preheat the oven to 200°C/400°F/
Gas 6. Brush a large ovenproof dish
with 15ml/1 tbsp of the oil.

2 Sprinkle the chopped flat leaf parsley
over the base of the dish and cover with
the beans. Cut the tomatoes into even
slices, discarding the two end slices of
each. Arrange the slices of tomato in
the dish over the beans so that they
overlap slightly. Sprinkle them with a
little salt and the sugar.

3 In a mixing bowl, stir together the
breadcrumbs, the remaining olive or
sunflower oil and chilli powder or
paprika, whichever you are using.

4 Sprinkle the crumb mixture over the
tomatoes, and bake in the oven for
50 minutes. Serve hot or cold,
garnished with chopped parsley and
accompanied by rye bread.

MIXED VEGETABLE CASSEROLE

THE VEGETABLES IN THIS RICH TOMATO SAUCE CAN BE VARIED ACCORDING TO SEASON.

SERVES FOUR

INGREDIENTS
1 aubergine (eggplant), diced into
   2.5cm/1in pieces
115g/4oz/½ cup okra, halved
   lengthways
115g/4oz/1 cup frozen or fresh peas
   or petits pois (baby peas)
115g/4oz/¾ cup green beans, cut
   into 2.5cm/1in pieces
400g/14oz can flageolet (small
   cannellini) beans, rinsed and drained
4 courgettes (zucchini), cut into
   1cm/½in pieces
2 onions, finely chopped
450g/1lb maincrop potatoes, diced
   into 2.5cm/1in pieces
1 red (bell) pepper, seeded and sliced
400g/14oz can chopped tomatoes
150ml/¼ pint/⅔ cup vegetable stock
60ml/4 tbsp olive oil
75ml/5 tbsp chopped fresh parsley
5ml/1 tsp paprika
salt
crusty bread, to serve
For the topping
   6 tomatoes, sliced
   1 courgette (zucchini), sliced

1 Slice the tomatoes and courgettes for
the topping.

2 Put all the other ingredients in an
ovenproof dish, combine them well.

3 Preheat the oven to 190°C/375°F/
Gas 5. Arrange alternate slices of
tomato and courgette attractively on the
top of the other vegetables.

4 Put the lid on or cover the casserole
tightly with foil. Bake in the oven for
60–70 minutes until all the vegetables
are tender. Remove the lid or foil for the
last 15 minutes to brown the topping
slightly, if you like. Serve either hot or
cold with wedges of crusty bread.

COOK'S TIP
For the finest flavour, use extra virgin
olive oil in the bake and vine-ripened or
home-grown tomatoes for the topping.

SPICY LEBANESE STEW

This is a traditional Lebanese dish that is popular all over the Mediterranean. Here the most is made of the wonderful combination of tomatoes and spices.

SERVES FOUR

INGREDIENTS
    3 large aubergines (eggplant), cubed
    200g/7oz/1 cup chickpeas, soaked
    60ml/4 tbsp olive oil
    3 garlic cloves, chopped
    2 large onions, chopped
    2.5ml/½ tsp ground cumin
    2.5ml/½ tsp ground cinnamon
    2.5ml/½ tsp ground coriander
    3 x 400g/14oz cans chopped
        tomatoes
    200g/7oz fresh tomatoes, chopped
    salt and ground black pepper
    cooked rice, to serve
For the garnish
    30ml/2 tbsp olive oil
    1 onion, sliced
    1 garlic clove, sliced
    fresh coriander (cilantro) sprigs

1 Place the aubergines in a colander and sprinkle them with salt. Stand the colander in the sink and leave for 30 minutes, to allow any bitter juices to escape. Rinse with cold water and dry on kitchen paper. Drain the chickpeas and put in a pan with enough water to cover. Bring to the boil and simmer for about 1 hour, or until tender. Drain.

2 Heat the oil in a large pan. Add the garlic and onions; cook gently, until soft. Add the spices and cook, stirring, for a few seconds. Stir in the aubergine and stir to coat with the spices and onion. Cook for 5 minutes. Add the tomatoes and chickpeas, and season with salt and pepper. Cover and simmer for 20 minutes.

3 To make the garnish, heat the oil in a frying pan and, when very hot, add the sliced onion and garlic. Fry until golden and crisp. Serve the stew with rice, topped with the onion and garlic, and garnished with coriander.

COOK'S TIPS
• Tender, young aubergines will not need to be salted.
• When fat, flavoursome beefsteak tomatoes are in the shops, use them instead of canned tomatoes. You will need about 6 large tomatoes.
• If you are in a hurry, substitute 2 cans of chickpeas for dried. Rinse and drain before adding to the tomato mixture, and cook for about 15 minutes.

CHICKPEA TAGINE

A TAGINE IS A TYPE OF MOROCCAN STEW ORIGINALLY PREPARED BY LONG SIMMERING OVER AN OPEN FIRE. A TAGINE CAN BE SAVOURY OR SWEET AND SOUR.

SERVES SIX TO EIGHT

INGREDIENTS

150g/5oz/⅔ cup chickpeas, soaked overnight, or 2 x 400g/14oz cans chickpeas, drained
30ml/2 tbsp sunflower oil or extra virgin olive oil
1 large onion, chopped
1 garlic clove, crushed or chopped (optional)
400g/14oz can chopped tomatoes
200g/7oz fresh tomatoes, peeled and puréed
5ml/1 tsp ground cumin
350ml/12fl oz/1½ cups vegetable stock
¼ preserved lemon
30ml/2 tbsp chopped fresh coriander (cilantro)
crusty bread, to serve

COOK'S TIP
To preserve lemons, quarter 6 unwaxed lemons and layer them with 90ml/6 tbsp sea salt in a sieve. Drain for 2 days, then pack in preserving jars with 30ml/2 tbsp black peppercorns, 4 bay leaves, 6 cardamom pods and a cinnamon stick. Cover with sunflower oil, seal and leave for 3–4 weeks before using.

1 If using dried chickpeas, drain and cook in plenty of boiling water for 1–1½ hours until tender. Drain again.

2 Skin the chickpeas by placing them in a bowl of cold water and rubbing them between your fingers – the skins will rise to the surface.

3 Heat the oil in a large pan or flameproof casserole and fry the onion and garlic, if using, for 8–10 minutes until golden.

4 Stir in the tomatoes and cumin, then pour over the stock and stir well. Cook for 10 minutes.

5 Add the chickpeas and simmer, uncovered, for 30–40 minutes more.

6 Rinse the preserved lemon and cut away the flesh and pith. Cut the peel into slivers and stir into the chickpeas along with the coriander. Serve immediately with crusty bread.

Tomatoes are just as delicious raw or cooked, so it is hardly surprising that they are used all over the world to add a splash of colour as well as a delicious flavour to an astonishingly wide variety of dishes. Cherry tomatoes add a sweet tangy bite to Moroccan Tuna and Tomato Salad with Beans and Eggs while plum tomatoes enhance the flavour of a Greek Salad. And if there's a glut of tomatoes, what better way to use them than in cooked dishes such as Spiced Potatoes and Tomatoes or classic Ratatouille.

Salads and
Side Dishes

ROASTED PEPPER AND TOMATO SALAD

THIS IS ONE OF THOSE LOVELY RECIPES THAT BRINGS TOGETHER PERFECTLY THE COLOURS, FLAVOURS AND TEXTURES OF SOUTHERN ITALIAN FOOD. EAT THIS DISH AT ROOM TEMPERATURE.

SERVES FOUR

INGREDIENTS

3 red (bell) peppers
6 large plum tomatoes
2.5ml/½ tsp dried red chilli flakes
1 red onion, finely sliced
3 garlic cloves, finely chopped
grated (shredded) rind and juice
  of 1 lemon
45ml/3 tbsp chopped fresh flat
  leaf parsley
30ml/2 tbsp extra virgin olive oil
salt
black and green olives and extra
  chopped flat leaf parsley, to garnish

COOK'S TIP
These peppers will keep for several weeks if the peeled pepper pieces are placed in a jar of olive oil, with a tight-fitting lid. Store in the refrigerator.

1 Preheat the oven to 220°C/425°F/Gas 7. Place the peppers on a baking sheet and roast for 10 minutes until the skins are slightly blackened. Add the tomatoes and bake for 5 minutes more.

2 Place the peppers in a plastic bag. Close the top loosely, trapping in the steam, and then set them aside, with the tomatoes, until they are cool.

3 Skin and seed the peppers. Chop the peppers and tomatoes roughly and place them both in a mixing bowl.

4 Add the chilli flakes, onion, garlic, lemon rind and juice. Sprinkle over the parsley. Mix well, then transfer to a serving dish. Season with salt, drizzle over the olive oil and sprinkle the olives and extra parsley over the top.

CHAYOTE <u>AND</u> TOMATO SALAD

COOL AND REFRESHING, THIS TOMATO SALAD IS IDEAL ON ITS OWN OR WITH FISH OR CHICKEN DISHES. THE SOFT FLESH OF THE CHAYOTES ABSORBS THE FLAVOUR OF THE DRESSING BEAUTIFULLY.

SERVES FOUR

INGREDIENTS
2 chayotes
2 firm tomatoes
1 small onion, finely chopped
finely sliced strips of fresh red and
  green chilli, to garnish
For the dressing
2.5ml/½ tsp Dijon mustard
2.5ml/½ tsp ground anise
90ml/6 tbsp white wine vinegar
60ml/4 tbsp olive oil
salt and ground black pepper

1 Bring a pan of water to the boil. Peel the chayotes, cut them in half and remove the seeds. Add them to the boiling water. Lower the heat and simmer for 20 minutes or until the chayotes are tender. Drain and set them aside to cool.

2 Meanwhile, skin the tomatoes by cutting a cross in the blossom end of each of them and plunging them into boiling water for 30 seconds. Lift the tomatoes out using a slotted spoon and drop them into a bowl of cold water. Drain. The skins will have begun to peel back from the crosses. Remove the skins completely and cut the tomatoes into wedges.

3 Make the dressing by combining all the ingredients in a screw-top jar. Close the lid tightly and then shake the jar vigorously to mix.

4 Cut the chayotes into wedges and place them in a bowl with the tomato and onion. Pour over the dressing and serve garnished with the strips of fresh red and green chilli.

GREEK SALAD

ANYONE WHO HAS SPENT A HOLIDAY IN GREECE WILL HAVE EATEN A VERSION OF THIS SALAD — THE GREEKS' EQUIVALENT OF A MIXED SALAD. ITS SUCCESS RELIES ON USING ONLY THE FRESHEST INGREDIENTS, INCLUDING SUN-RIPENED TOMATOES, AND A GOOD OLIVE OIL.

SERVES SIX

INGREDIENTS
 450g/1lb well-flavoured plum
  tomatoes, skinned
 1 small cos (romaine) lettuce, sliced
 1 cucumber, seeded and chopped
 200g/7oz feta cheese, crumbled
 4 spring onions (scallions), sliced
 50g/2oz/½ cup pitted black
  olives, halved
For the dressing
 90ml/6 tbsp extra virgin olive oil
 25ml/1½ tbsp lemon juice
 salt and ground black pepper

1 Place the tomatoes on a chopping board. Using a sharp cook's knife or a serrated knife, cut into quarters and then into eighths. Put them in a bowl and add the lettuce, cucumber, feta, spring onions and olives.

2 Make the dressing. In a bowl, whisk together the olive oil and lemon juice, then season with salt and ground black pepper, and whisk again. Pour the dressing over the salad. Mix well and serve immediately.

SPICED TOMATO SALAD

SERVE THIS MIDDLE-EASTERN INFLUENCED SALAD WITH WARM PITTA BREAD AS AN APPETIZER OR TO ACCOMPANY A MAIN-COURSE RICE PILAFF. IT IS ALSO GREAT WITH FLAME-GRILLED MEATS.

SERVES FOUR

INGREDIENTS
 2 small aubergines (eggplant), sliced
 75ml/5 tbsp olive oil
 60ml/4 tbsp red wine vinegar
 2 garlic cloves, crushed
 15ml/1 tbsp lemon juice
 2.5ml/½ tsp ground cumin
 2.5ml/½ tsp ground coriander
 7 well-flavoured tomatoes
 ½ cucumber
 30ml/2 tbsp natural (plain) yogurt
 salt and ground black pepper
 chopped flat leaf parsley, to garnish

VARIATION
An equally delicious warm salad can be made by dicing the aubergines, then frying them in olive oil with 1 chopped onion and 2 crushed garlic cloves. Stir in 5–10ml/1–2 tsp mild curry powder and 3 chopped tomatoes. Cook until soft. Serve with natural yogurt.

1 Preheat the grill (broiler). Brush all the aubergine slices lightly with some of the oil and cook under a high heat, turning once, until golden and tender. Cut each slice into quarters.

2 In a bowl, mix together the remaining oil, vinegar, garlic, lemon juice, cumin and coriander. Season with salt and pepper, and mix thoroughly. Add the warm aubergines, stir well and chill for at least 2 hours.

3 Using a sharp knife, slice, or if you prefer, cut the tomatoes into quarters. Slice the cucumber finely, leaving the seeds intact. Add both cucumber and tomato to the aubergine mixture.

4 Transfer the salad vegetables to an attractive serving dish and arrange them decoratively. Spoon the natural yogurt over the aubergine mixture. Sprinkle with the freshly chopped flat leaf parsley and serve.

Moroccan Tuna <u>and</u> Tomato Salad <u>with</u> Beans <u>and</u> Eggs

This salad is similar to the classic salad Niçoise and uses tuna or swordfish steaks, with green beans, cherry tomatoes and a herb and spice marinade.

SERVES SIX

INGREDIENTS
    6 tuna or swordfish steaks, about
      900g/2lb total weight
For the marinade
    1 onion
    2 garlic cloves, halved
    ½ bunch fresh parsley
    ½ bunch fresh coriander (cilantro)
    10ml/2 tsp paprika
    45ml/3 tbsp olive oil
    30ml/2 tbsp white wine vinegar
    15ml/1 tbsp lime or lemon juice
For the salad
    450g/1lb green beans
    450g/1lb broad (fava) beans
    1 cos (romaine) lettuce
    450g/1lb cherry tomatoes, halved
    30ml/2 tbsp coarsely chopped fresh
      coriander (cilantro)
    3 hard-boiled (hard-cooked) eggs
    45ml/3 tbsp extra virgin olive oil
    10–15ml/2–3 tsp lime or lemon juice
    ½ garlic clove, crushed
    175–225g/6–8oz/1½–2 cups pitted
      black olives

1 First make the marinade. Skin and cut the onion into quarters or eighths. Place the onion, garlic, parsley, coriander, paprika, olive oil, wine vinegar and lime or lemon juice in a food processor, add 45ml/3 tbsp water and process for 30–40 seconds until all the ingredients are finely chopped.

2 Prick the tuna or swordfish steaks all over with a fork, place in a shallow dish that is large enough to hold them in a single layer and pour over the marinade, turning the fish so that each piece is coated. Cover and leave in a cool place for 2–4 hours.

3 To prepare the salad, cook the green beans and broad beans in boiling salted water for 5–10 minutes or until tender. Drain, refresh in cold running water and drain again.

4 Discard the outer shells from the broad beans and place them in a large serving bowl with the green beans. Remove the outer leaves from the lettuce and tear the inner leaves into pieces. Add to the bowl with the tomatoes and coriander.

5 Shell the eggs and cut into eighths with a sharp knife. To make the dressing, whisk the olive oil, citrus juice and garlic in a bowl.

6 Preheat the grill (broiler) and arrange the fish steaks on a grill pan. Brush with the marinade mixed with a little extra olive oil and grill (broil) for 5–6 minutes on each side, until tender. Brush with marinade and more olive oil when turning the fish over.

7 Allow the fish to cool a little and then break the steaks into large pieces. Toss into the salad with the olives and dressing. Add the eggs and serve.

WARM CHICKEN AND TOMATO SALAD WITH HAZELNUT DRESSING

THIS SIMPLE, WARM SALAD COMBINES PAN-FRIED CHICKEN AND SPINACH WITH A LIGHT, NUTTY DRESSING. SERVE IT FOR LUNCH ON AN AUTUMN DAY.

SERVES FOUR

INGREDIENTS

45ml/3 tbsp olive oil
30ml/2 tbsp hazelnut oil
15ml/1 tbsp white wine vinegar
1 garlic clove, crushed
15ml/1 tbsp chopped fresh mixed herbs
225g/8oz baby spinach leaves
250g/9oz cherry tomatoes, halved
1 bunch spring onions
   (scallions), chopped
2 skinless, boneless chicken breasts,
   cut into thin strips
salt and ground black pepper

VARIATIONS

• Use other meat or fish, such as steak, pork fillet or salmon fillet, in place of the chicken breasts.
• Any salad leaves can be used instead of the baby spinach.

1 First make the dressing: place 30ml/ 2 tbsp of the olive oil, the hazelnut oil, vinegar, garlic and chopped herbs in a small bowl or jug and whisk together until thoroughly mixed. Set aside.

2 Trim any long stalks from the spinach leaves, then place in a large serving bowl with the tomatoes and spring onions, and toss together to mix.

3 Heat the remaining olive oil in a frying pan, and stir-fry the chicken over a high heat for 7–10 minutes until it is cooked, tender and lightly browned.

4 Arrange the cooked chicken pieces over the salad. Give the dressing a quick whisk to blend, then drizzle it over the salad. Add salt and pepper to taste, toss lightly and serve immediately.

PANZANELLA

IN THIS LIVELY ITALIAN SPECIALITY, A SWEET TANGY BLEND OF TOMATO JUICE, RICH OLIVE OIL AND RED WINE VINEGAR MAKES A MARVELLOUS DRESSING FOR A COLOURFUL SALAD.

SERVES FOUR TO SIX

INGREDIENTS
225g/8oz ciabatta
150ml/¼ pint/⅔ cup extra virgin
  olive oil
3 red (bell) peppers
3 yellow (bell) peppers
50g/2oz can anchovy fillets
675g/1½lb ripe plum tomatoes
4 garlic cloves, crushed
60ml/4 tbsp red wine vinegar
50g/2oz/⅓ cup capers, drained
115g/4oz/1 cup pitted black olives
salt and ground black pepper
fresh basil leaves, to garnish

1 Preheat the grill (broiler) and line the pan with foil. Also preheat the oven to 200ºC/400ºF/Gas 6. Cut the ciabatta into 2cm/¾in chunks and drizzle with 60ml/4 tbsp of the oil. Place on the lined grill pan and grill (broil) lightly until just golden. Set aside.

2 Put the peppers on a foil-lined baking sheet and bake for about 45 minutes, turning them occasionally, until the skins begin to char. Remove from the oven, cover with a dishtowel and leave to cool slightly.

3 Skin and quarter the peppers, remove the stalk and seeds. Drain and then roughly chop the anchovies. Set aside. Halve the tomatoes and scoop the seeds into a sieve set over a bowl.

4 Using the back of a spoon, press the tomato pulp in the sieve to extract as much juice as possible. Discard the pulp and add the remaining oil, the garlic and vinegar to the juices.

5 Layer the bread, peppers, tomatoes, anchovies; capers and olives in a salad bowl. Season the tomato dressing and pour it over the salad. Leave to stand for about 30 minutes. Serve garnished with plenty of basil leaves.

GREEN BEANS WITH TOMATOES

THIS RECIPE IS FULL OF THE FLAVOURS OF SUMMER. IT RELIES ON FIRST-CLASS INGREDIENTS, SO USE ONLY THE BEST RIPE PLUM TOMATOES AND GREEN BEANS THAT YOU CAN BUY.

SERVES FOUR

INGREDIENTS

30ml/2 tbsp olive oil
1 large onion, finely sliced
2 garlic cloves, finely chopped
6 large ripe plum tomatoes, peeled, seeded and coarsely chopped
150ml/¼ pint/⅔ cup dry white wine
450g/1lb green beans, sliced in half lengthways
16 pitted black olives
10ml/2 tsp lemon juice
salt and ground black pepper

COOK'S TIP
Green beans need little preparation, and now that they are grown without the string, you simply trim either end.

1 Heat the oil in a large frying pan. Add the finely sliced onion and chopped garlic. Cook over a medium heat for about 5 minutes, stirring frequently and lowering the heat if necessary, until the onion has softened but not browned.

2 Add the chopped tomatoes, white wine, beans, olives and lemon juice, and cook over a gentle heat for a further 20 minutes, stirring occasionally, until the sauce has thickened and the beans are tender. Season with salt and pepper to taste and serve immediately.

SPICY ROASTED VEGETABLES

OVEN ROASTING BRINGS OUT ALL THE FLAVOURS OF CHERRY TOMATOES, COURGETTES (ZUCCHINI), ONION AND RED PEPPERS. SERVE THEM HOT WITH MEAT OR FISH.

SERVES FOUR

INGREDIENTS

2–3 courgettes (zucchini)
1 Spanish onion
2 red (bell) peppers
16 cherry tomatoes
2 garlic cloves, chopped
pinch of cumin seeds
5ml/1 tsp fresh thyme or 4–5 torn
  fresh basil leaves
60ml/4 tbsp olive oil
juice of ½ lemon
5–10ml/1–2 tsp harissa or
  Tabasco sauce
fresh thyme sprigs, to garnish

COOK'S TIP
Harissa is a chilli paste, popular in northern Africa. It can be bought in cans and contains pounded chillies, garlic, coriander, olive oil and seasoning.

1 Preheat the oven to 220°C/425°F/ Gas 7. Trim the courgettes and cut into long strips. Cut the onion into thin wedges. Cut the peppers into chunks, discarding the seeds and core.

2 Place these vegetables in a cast-iron dish or roasting tin (pan); add the tomatoes, chopped garlic, cumin seeds and thyme or torn basil leaves.

3 Sprinkle with the olive oil and toss to coat. Cook the mixture in the oven for 25–30 minutes until the vegetables are very soft and have begun to char slightly.

4 In a cup, mix the lemon juice with the harissa or Tabasco sauce. Stir into the vegetables, garnish with the thyme and serve immediately.

SPICED POTATOES <u>AND</u> TOMATOES

SUBSTANTIAL ENOUGH TO SERVE SOLO, THIS DISH CONSISTS OF DICED POTATOES COOKED GENTLY IN A FRESH TOMATO SAUCE, WHICH IS FLAVOURED WITH CURRY LEAVES AND GREEN CHILLIES.

SERVES FOUR

INGREDIENTS
- 2 medium potatoes
- 15ml/1 tbsp olive oil
- 2 medium onions, finely chopped
- 4 curry leaves
- 1.5ml/¼ tsp onion seeds
- 1 fresh green chilli, seeded and finely chopped
- 4 tomatoes, sliced
- 5ml/1 tsp grated fresh root ginger
- 1 garlic clove, crushed
- 5ml/1 tsp chilli powder
- 5ml/1 tsp ground coriander
- 5ml/1 tsp lemon juice
- 15ml/1 tbsp chopped fresh coriander (cilantro)
- 3 hard-boiled (hard-cooked) eggs

1 Peel and dice the potatoes. Heat the oil in a non-stick wok or frying pan and stir-fry the onions, curry leaves, onion seeds and chilli for about 1 minute.

2 Add the tomatoes and cook for about 2 minutes over a low heat, shaking the pan to prevent them from sticking.

3 Add the ginger, garlic, chilli powder, ground coriander and salt to taste. Continue to stir-fry for 1–2 minutes, then add the potatoes and cover the pan. Cook over a low heat for 5–7 minutes until the potatoes are tender.

4 Add the lemon juice and fresh coriander, and stir to mix together.

5 Shell the hard-boiled eggs, cut into quarters and add as a garnish to the finished dish.

BAKED CABBAGE AND TOMATOES

THIS ECONOMICAL DISH USES THE WHOLE CABBAGE, INCLUDING THE CORE WHERE MUCH OF THE FLAVOUR RESIDES. THE TOMATO TOPPING KEEPS THE CABBAGE BEAUTIFULLY MOIST.

SERVES FOUR

INGREDIENTS

1 green or white cabbage, about
  675g/1½lb
15ml/1 tbsp olive oil
45–60ml/3–4 tbsp vegetable or
  chicken stock
4 firm ripe tomatoes, peeled
  and chopped
5ml/1 tsp mild chilli powder
salt and ground black pepper
15ml/1 tbsp chopped fresh parsley or
  fennel, to garnish (optional)
For the topping
3 firm ripe tomatoes, thinly sliced
15ml/1 tbsp extra virgin olive oil
  or nut oil

1 Preheat the oven to 180°C/350°F/ Gas 4. Finely shred the leaves and the core of the cabbage. Heat the oil in a frying pan with 30ml/2 tbsp water and add the cabbage. Cook over a very low heat, to allow the cabbage to sweat, for about 5–10 minutes with the lid on. Stir occasionally.

2 Add the stock and then stir in the chopped tomatoes. Cook for a further 10 minutes. Add the chilli powder and a little salt to season. Cook for 2–3 minutes, stirring occasionally.

3 Tip the cabbage mixture into the base of an ovenproof dish. Level the surface of the cabbage and arrange the sliced tomatoes on top. Season and brush with the oil to prevent them from drying out. Cook for 30–40 minutes, or until the tomatoes are just starting to brown. Serve hot, garnished with a little parsley or fennel sprinkled over the top, if you like.

VARIATION
• Add seeded, diced red or green (bell) peppers to the cabbage with the tomatoes.
• For those who do not like spicy food, this dish is just as delicious without chilli.

RATATOUILLE

A HIGHLY VERSATILE TOMATO AND MIXED VEGETABLE STEW FROM PROVENCE, FRANCE, RATATOUILLE IS DELICIOUS WARM OR COLD, ON ITS OWN OR WITH EGGS, PASTA, FISH OR MEAT — PARTICULARLY LAMB.

SERVES SIX

INGREDIENTS

- 900g/2lb ripe tomatoes
- 120ml/4fl oz/½ cup olive oil
- 2 onions, thinly sliced
- 2 red and 1 yellow (bell) pepper, seeded and cut into chunks
- 1 large aubergine (eggplant), cut into chunks
- 2 courgettes (zucchini), sliced
- 4 garlic cloves, crushed
- 2 bay leaves
- 15ml/1 tbsp chopped thyme
- salt and ground black pepper

1 Plunge the tomatoes into boiling water for 30 seconds, then refresh in cold water. Peel away the skins and chop the flesh roughly.

2 Heat a little of the olive oil in a large, heavy pan and gently fry the onions for 5 minutes. Stir them constantly so that they do not brown, as this will adversely affect their flavour and make them bitter, but cook them until they are just transparent.

3 Add the peppers to the fried onions and cook for a further 2 minutes. Using a slotted spoon, transfer the onions and peppers to a plate and set them aside.

4 Add more oil and the aubergine and fry gently for 5 minutes. Add the remaining oil and courgettes, and fry for 3 minutes. Lift out the courgettes and aubergine and set them aside.

5 Add the garlic and tomatoes to the pan with the bay leaves and thyme, and a little salt and pepper. Cook gently until the tomatoes have softened and are turning pulpy.

6 Return all the vegetables to the pan and cook gently, stirring frequently, for about 15 minutes, until fairly pulpy but retaining a little texture. Season to taste. Serve warm or cold.

To give savoury dishes a kick, serve some salsa — from
mild and fruity Guacamole to Fragrant Roasted Tomato
Salsa, there are many variations on the basic theme. As
for cold meats and cheeses, they become much more
interesting when served with a dollop of Tomato Chutney
or a spoonful of Tart Tomato Relish. Tomatoes add a twist
to delicious home-made bread — for a real treat make
Sun-dried Tomato Bread and eat it straight from the
oven with butter.

Salsas, Dips, Relishes and Breads

FRESH TOMATO <u>AND</u> TARRAGON SALSA

PLUM TOMATOES, GARLIC, OLIVE OIL AND BALSAMIC VINEGAR MAKE FOR A VERY MEDITERRANEAN SALSA — TRY SERVING THIS WITH GRILLED LAMB CUTLETS OR TOSS IT WITH FRESHLY COOKED PASTA.

SERVES FOUR

INGREDIENTS
    8 plum tomatoes, or 500g/1¼lb
      sweet cherry tomatoes
    1 small garlic clove
    60ml/4 tbsp olive oil or
      sunflower oil
    15ml/1 tbsp balsamic vinegar
    30ml/2 tbsp chopped fresh tarragon,
      plus extra shredded leaves,
      to garnish
    salt and ground black pepper

1 Plunge the tomatoes into boiling water for 30 seconds. Remove with a slotted spoon; cool in cold water.

2 Slip off the tomato skins and finely chop the flesh.

3 Using a sharp knife, crush or finely chop the garlic.

4 Whisk together the oil, balsamic vinegar and plenty of salt and pepper.

5 Add the chopped fresh tarragon to the oil mixture.

6 Mix the tomatoes and garlic in a bowl and pour the tarragon dressing over. Leave to infuse (steep) for at least 1 hour before serving at room temperature. Garnish with shredded tarragon leaves.

COOK'S TIP
Be sure to serve this salsa at room temperature as the tomatoes taste less sweet, and rather acidic, when chilled.

GRILLED CORN-ON-THE-COB SALSA

THIS IS AN UNUSUAL SALSA AND CONTAINS DELICIOUSLY SWEET VEGETABLES. USE CHERRY TOMATOES FOR AN EXTRA SPECIAL FLAVOUR, AND COMBINE WITH THE RIPEST AND FRESHEST CORN ON THE COB.

SERVES FOUR

INGREDIENTS

2 corn on the cob
30ml/2 tbsp melted butter
4 tomatoes
8 spring onions (scallions)
1 garlic clove
30ml/2 tbsp fresh lemon juice
30ml/2 tbsp olive oil
Tabasco sauce, to taste

1 Remove the husks and silky threads covering the corn on the cob. Brush the cobs with the melted butter and gently cook on the barbecue or grill (broil) them for 20–30 minutes, turning occasionally, until tender and tinged brown.

2 To remove the kernels, stand each cob upright on a chopping board and use a large, heavy knife to slice down the length of the cob.

3 Plunge the tomatoes into boiling water for 30 seconds. Remove with a slotted spoon; cool in cold water. Slip off the skins and dice the tomato flesh.

4 Place 6 spring onions on a chopping board and chop finely. Crush and chop the garlic and then mix together with the corn and tomato in a small bowl.

5 Stir the lemon juice and olive oil together, adding Tabasco sauce, salt and pepper to taste.

6 Pour this mixture over the salsa and stir well. Cover the salsa and leave to steep at room temperature for 1–2 hours before serving. Garnish with the remaining spring onions.

COOK'S TIP
Make this salsa in summer when fresh cobs of corn are readily available.

CLASSIC TOMATO SALSA

This is the traditional tomato-based salsa that most people associate with Mexican food. There are innumerable recipes for it, but the basic ingredients of onion, tomato and chilli are common to every one of them. Serve this salsa as a condiment. It goes well with a wide variety of dishes.

SERVES SIX AS AN ACCOMPANIMENT

INGREDIENTS

  3–6 fresh Serrano chillies
  1 large white onion
  grated (shredded) rind and juice of
    2 limes, plus strips of lime rind,
    to garnish
  8 ripe, firm tomatoes
  large bunch of fresh coriander (cilantro)
  1.5ml/¼ tsp sugar
  salt

VARIATIONS
• Use spring onions (scallions) or mild red onions instead of white onion.
• For a smoky flavour, use chipotle chillies instead of Serrano chillies.

1 Use 3 chillies for a salsa of medium heat; up to 6 if you like it hot. To peel the chillies, spear them on a long-handled metal skewer and roast them over the flame of a gas burner until the skins blister and darken. Do not let the flesh burn. Alternatively, dry-fry them in a griddle pan until the skins are scorched.

2 Place the roasted chillies in a strong plastic bag and tie the top of the bag to keep the steam in. Set aside for about 20 minutes.

3 Meanwhile, chop the onion finely and put it in a bowl with the lime rind and juice. The lime juice will soften the onion considerably.

4 Remove the chillies from the bag and peel off the skins. Cut off the stalks, then slit the chillies and scrape out the seeds. Chop the flesh and set it aside in a small bowl.

5 Cut a small cross in the base of each tomato. Place in a heatproof bowl and pour over boiling water to cover.

6 Lift out the tomatoes and plunge them into a bowl of cold water. Drain well. Remove the skins.

7 Dice the peeled tomatoes and put them in a bowl. Add the chopped onion, which should by now have softened, together with any remaining lime juice and rind. Chop the coriander finely.

8 Add the chopped coriander to the salsa, with the chillies and the sugar. Mix gently until the sugar has dissolved and all the ingredients are coated in lime juice. Cover and chill for 2–3 hours to allow the flavours to blend. Garnish with the extra strips of lime rind just before serving.

COOK'S TIP
The salsa can be made ahead of time. The flavour will intensify on keeping. Scrape the salsa into a jar and cover tightly, or simply cover the bowl with a double thickness of clear film. Store in the refrigerator for 3–4 days.

FRAGRANT ROASTED TOMATO SALSA

ROASTING THE TOMATOES GIVES A GREATER DEPTH TO THE FLAVOUR OF THIS SALSA, WHICH ALSO BENEFITS FROM THE WARM, ROUNDED FLAVOUR OF ROASTED CHILLIES.

SERVES SIX AS AN ACCOMPANIMENT

INGREDIENTS
  500g/1¼lb tomatoes, preferably
    beefsteak tomatoes
  2 fresh Serrano chillies or other fresh
    red chillies
  1 onion
  juice of 1 lime
  large bunch of fresh coriander (cilantro)
  salt

1 Preheat the oven to 200°C/400°F/ Gas 6. Cut the tomatoes into quarters and place them in a roasting pan. Add the chillies. Roast for 45 minutes to 1 hour, until the tomatoes and chillies are charred and softened.

2 Place the roasted chillies in a strong plastic bag. Tie the top to keep the steam in and set aside for 20 minutes. Leave the tomatoes to cool slightly, then use a small, sharp knife to remove the skins and dice the flesh.

3 Chop the onion finely, then place it in a bowl and add the lime juice and the diced tomatoes. Mix well with a wooden spoon.

4 Remove the chillies from the bag and peel off the skins. Cut off the stalks, then slit the chillies and scrape out the seeds with a sharp knife. Chop the chillies roughly and add them to the onion mixture. Mix well.

5 Chop the coriander and add most of it to the salsa. Add salt to season, cover and chill for at least 1 hour before serving, sprinkled with the remaining chopped coriander. This salsa will keep in the refrigerator for 1 week.

GUACAMOLE

ONE OF THE BEST-LOVED MEXICAN SALSAS, THIS BLEND OF CREAMY AVOCADO, TOMATOES, CHILLIES, CORIANDER AND LIME NOW APPEARS ON TABLES THE WORLD OVER. BOUGHT GUACAMOLE USUALLY CONTAINS MAYONNAISE, WHICH HELPS TO PRESERVE THE AVOCADO, BUT THIS IS NOT AN INGREDIENT THAT YOU ARE LIKELY TO FIND IN TRADITIONAL RECIPES.

SERVES SIX TO EIGHT

INGREDIENTS
4 tomatoes
4 ripe avocados, preferably *fuerte*
juice of 1 lime
½ small onion
2 garlic cloves
small bunch of fresh coriander
  (cilantro), chopped
3 fresh red fresno chillies
salt
tortilla chips or breadsticks, to serve

COOK'S TIP
Smooth-skinned *fuerte* avocados are native to Mexico, so would be ideal for this dip. If they are not available, use any avocados, but make sure they are ripe. To test, gently press the top of the avocado; it should give a little.

1 Cut a cross in the base of each tomato. Place the tomatoes in a heatproof bowl and pour over boiling water to cover. The easiest way to do this is to use a kettle, but some people prefer just a pan of boiling water.

2 Leave the tomatoes in the water for 30 seconds, then lift them out using a slotted spoon and plunge them into a bowl of cold water. Drain. The skins will have begun to peel back from the crosses. Remove the skins completely. Cut the tomatoes in half, remove the seeds with a teaspoon, then chop the flesh roughly and set it aside.

3 Cut the avocados in half then remove the stones (pits). Scoop the flesh out of the shells and place it in a food processor or blender. Process until almost smooth, then scrape into a bowl and stir in the freshly squeezed lime juice.

4 Chop the onion finely, then crush the garlic. Add both to the avocado and mix well. Stir in the coriander.

5 Remove the stalks from the chillies, slit them and scrape out the seeds with a small, sharp knife. Chop the chillies finely and add them to the avocado mixture, with the roughly chopped tomatoes. Mix well.

6 Taste the guacamole and add salt if needed. Cover closely with clear film or a tight-fitting lid and chill for 1 hour before serving as a dip with tortilla chips or breadsticks. If it is well covered, guacamole will keep in the refrigerator for 2–3 days.

TOMATO CHUTNEY

This spicy chutney is delicious served with a selection of cheeses and crackers, or with cold meats. It is very good with baked ham.

MAKES ABOUT 1.8KG/4LB

INGREDIENTS
    900g/2lb tomatoes
    225g/8oz/1⅓ cups raisins
    225g/8oz onions, chopped
    225g/8oz/1 cup caster
     (superfine) sugar
    600ml/1 pint/2½ cups malt vinegar

COOK'S TIPS
• Tomatoes make good chutney and it is interesting to compare the difference in flavour between that made with ripe red tomatoes and green tomatoes.
• The chutney will keep, unopened, for up to a year. Once opened, store in the refrigerator and consume within a week.

1 Put the tomatoes in a heatproof bowl and pour over boiling water to cover. Leave for 30 seconds, then lift out each tomato in turn with a slotted spoon and place in a bowl of cold water. Drain, then slip off the skins.

2 Chop the tomatoes roughly. Put them in a preserving pan or a large, heavy pan.

3 Add the raisins, onions and caster sugar to the pan.

4 Pour over the vinegar. Bring to the boil, then reduce the heat and let the mixture simmer for 2 hours, uncovered. Spoon the hot chutney into warm sterilized jars. Seal each jar with a waxed circle and cover with a tightly fitting cellophane top. Store in a cool, dark place for at least 1 month before using.

TART TOMATO RELISH

THE WHOLE LIME USED IN THIS RECIPE ADDS A PLEASANTLY SOUR AFTERTASTE. SERVE THIS TASTY RELISH WITH GRILLED OR ROAST PORK OR LAMB. IT ALSO GOES WELL WITH OILY FISH, LIKE MACKEREL.

SERVES FOUR

INGREDIENTS

2 pieces preserved stem ginger
1 lime
450g/1lb cherry tomatoes
115g/4oz/½ cup light brown sugar
105ml/7 tbsp white wine vinegar
5ml/1 tsp salt

COOK'S TIP
Jars of this relish make marvellous presents at any time of the year. Next time you are invited to dinner, take along some tart tomato relish instead of the customary bottle of wine and see how welcome it will be. Label the jar with the contents, and don't forget the storage instructions.

1 Coarsely chop the ginger. Slice the whole lime thinly, then chop it into small pieces; do not remove the rind.

2 Place the whole cherry tomatoes, sugar, vinegar, salt, ginger and lime in a pan.

3 Bring to the boil, stirring until the sugar dissolves, then simmer rapidly for 45 minutes. Stir regularly until the liquid has evaporated and the relish is thickened and pulpy.

4 Allow the relish to cool for about 5 minutes, then spoon it into clean jars. Cool completely, cover and store in the refrigerator for up to 1 month. Spoon into a bowl to serve.

SUN-DRIED TOMATO BREAD

IN THE SOUTH OF ITALY, TOMATOES ARE OFTEN DRIED IN THE HOT SUN. THEY ARE THEN PRESERVED IN OIL, OR HUNG UP IN STRINGS IN THE KITCHEN, FOR USE IN THE WINTER. THIS RECIPE USES THE TYPE IN OIL TO MAKE FOUR DELICIOUS LOAVES.

MAKES FOUR SMALL LOAVES

INGREDIENTS
    675g/1½lb/6 cups strong white
      (bread) flour, plus extra for dusting
    10ml/2 tsp salt
    30ml/2 tbsp sugar
    25g/1oz fresh yeast
    400–475ml/14–16fl oz/1⅔–2 cups
      warm milk
    15ml/1 tbsp tomato purée (paste)
    75g/3oz/1½ cups sun-dried
      tomatoes, drained and chopped,
      plus 75ml/5 tbsp oil from the jar
    75ml/5 tbsp extra virgin olive oil, or
      sunflower oil
    1 large onion, finely chopped

COOK'S TIP
Use a pair of sharp kitchen scissors to
cut up the sun-dried tomatoes – serrated
ones work best.

1 Sift the flour, salt and sugar into a bowl, and make a well in the centre. Crumble the yeast, mix with 150ml/¼ pint/⅔ cup of the warm milk and add to the flour.

2 Mix the tomato purée into the remaining milk, until evenly blended, then add to the flour with the tomato oil and olive oil.

3 Gradually mix the flour into the liquid ingredients, until you have a dough. Turn out on to a floured work surface, and knead for about 10 minutes, until the dough is smooth and elastic.

4 Return the dough to the clean bowl, cover with a clean dishtowel or clear film and leave to rise in a warm place for about 2 hours.

5 Punch the dough back down, and add the tomatoes and onion. Knead until evenly distributed through the dough. Shape into four rounds and place on a greased baking sheet. Cover with a dishtowel and leave in a warm place to rise again for about 45 minutes.

6 Preheat the oven to 190ºC/375ºF/Gas 5. Bake the bread for 45 minutes, or until the loaves sound hollow when you tap them underneath with your fingers. Leave to cool on a wire rack. Eat warm or cut into thick slices and toast. Serve with mozzarella cheese grated on top, if liked.

HERBY TOMATO BREAD

This mouthwatering Italian-style bread, flavoured with basil, rosemary, olive oil and sun-dried tomatoes, is absolutely delicious served warm with a fresh salad and sliced salami or prosciutto. The olive oil, as well as adding flavour, helps it to keep longer.

MAKES THREE LOAVES

INGREDIENTS

50g/2oz/½ cup sun-dried tomatoes, drained
fresh rosemary and basil, or other fresh herbs
5ml/1 tsp sugar
900ml/1½ pints/3¾ cups warm water
15ml/1 tbsp dried yeast
1.3kg/3lb/12 cups strong white (bread) flour
15ml/1 tbsp salt
150ml/¼ pint/⅔ cup extra virgin olive oil or grapeseed oil
extra virgin olive oil, rosemary leaves and sea salt flakes, to garnish

COOK'S TIP
Use a sharp cook's knife to slash the tops of the loaves just before the final rising. Make a criss-cross pattern, cutting about 1cm/½in deep.

1 Put the sun-dried tomatoes on a board and chop them roughly. Strip the leaves from the rosemary and chop them with enough fresh basil to yield about 75ml/5 tbsp altogether.

2 Put the sugar into a small bowl, pour on 150ml/¼ pint/⅔ cup of the warm water, then crumble the yeast over the top. Leave in a warm place for 10–15 minutes, until frothy. Put the flour, salt, herbs and sun-dried tomatoes into a large bowl. Add the oil and frothy yeast mixture, then gradually mix in the remaining warm water.

3 As the mixture becomes stiffer, bring it together with your hands. Mix to a soft but not sticky dough, adding a little extra water if needed. Turn the dough out on to a lightly floured work surface and knead for 5 minutes until smooth and elastic. Put the dough back into the bowl, cover it loosely with oiled clear film and put in a warm place for 30–40 minutes or until doubled in bulk.

4 Knead again, then cut into 3 pieces. Shape each into an oval loaf and place on oiled baking sheets. Slash the top of each loaf. Loosely cover and leave in a warm place for 15–20 minutes until well risen. Preheat the oven to 220°C/425°F/Gas 7. Brush the loaves with a little olive oil and sprinkle with rosemary leaves and salt flakes. Bake for 25–30 minutes.

FOCACCIA WITH SUN-DRIED TOMATOES

A DIMPLED SURFACE IS FOCACCIA'S FAMOUS TRADEMARK. THIS VERSION MAKES A WONDERFUL TOMATO SANDWICH, OR TRY IT TOASTED, WITH COOKED TOMATOES ON TOP.

SERVES EIGHT

INGREDIENTS
    300ml/½ pint/1¼ cups warm water
    5ml/1 tsp dried yeast
    pinch of caster (superfine) sugar
    450g/1lb /4 cups strong white
      (bread) flour, plus extra for dusting
    5ml/1 tsp salt
    1.5ml/¼ tsp ground black pepper
    15ml/1 tbsp pesto
    115g/4oz/1 cup black olives, chopped
    25g/1oz/3 tbsp drained sun-dried
      tomatoes in oil, chopped, plus
      15ml/1 tbsp oil from the jar
    5ml/1 tsp coarse sea salt
    5ml/1 tsp roughly chopped
      fresh rosemary

1 Lightly grease a 33 x 23cm/13 x 9in baking tray. Put the water in a bowl. Sprinkle the yeast on top. Add the sugar, mix well and leave for 10 minutes.

2 Sift the flour, salt and pepper into a bowl and make a well in the centre. Add the yeast mixture with the pesto, olives and sun-dried tomatoes.

3 Mix to a soft dough, adding a little extra water if necessary. Turn the dough on to a floured surface and knead for 5 minutes until smooth and elastic.

4 Return the bread dough to a clean bowl, cover with a clean damp dishtowel or oiled plastic and leave in a warm place to rise for about 2 hours, or until doubled in bulk. Preheat the oven to 220°C/425°F/Gas 7.

5 Turn the dough on to a floured surface, knead briefly, then roll out to a 33 x 23cm/13 x 9in rectangle. Place in the prepared tray.

6 Using your fingertips, dimple the dough. Brush with the oil from the sun-dried tomatoes, then sprinkle with the salt and rosemary. Leave to rise for 20 minutes, then bake for 20–25 minutes, or until golden. Serve warm.

SUN-DRIED TOMATO LOAF

THERE'S SOMETHING VERY APPEALING ABOUT A BRAIDED LOAF. RED PESTO, PARMESAN AND SUN-DRIED TOMATOES MAKE THIS ONE EXTRA SPECIAL.

SERVES EIGHT TO TEN

INGREDIENTS

300ml/½ pint/1¼ cups warm water
5ml/1 tsp dried yeast
pinch of sugar
225g/8 oz/2 cups wholemeal
 (whole-wheat) flour
225g/8oz/2 cups strong white
 (bread) flour, plus extra for dusting
5ml/1 tsp salt
1.5ml/¼ tsp ground black pepper
115g/4oz/1 cup drained sun-dried
 tomatoes in oil, plus 15ml/1 tbsp
 oil from the jar
25g/1oz/⅓ cup freshly grated
 (shredded) Parmesan cheese
30ml/2 tbsp red pesto
5ml/1 tsp coarse sea salt

COOK'S TIP

These two breads can be made using easy-blend (rapid-rise) dried yeast. Mix all the dry ingredients, including the yeast, then add the lukewarm water. Mix to a dough, working in any other ingredients.

1 Put half the warm water in a bowl. Sprinkle the yeast on top. Add the sugar, mix well and leave to stand for about 10 minutes.

2 Put the wholemeal flour in a mixing bowl. Sift in the white flour, salt and pepper. Make a well in the centre and add the yeast mixture, sun-dried tomatoes, oil, Parmesan, pesto and the remaining water. Gradually incorporate the flour and mix to a soft dough, adding a little extra water if necessary.

3 Turn the dough on to a floured surface and knead for 5 minutes until smooth and elastic. Return to the clean bowl, cover with a clean, damp dishtowel and leave in a warm place to rise for about 2 hours until doubled in bulk. Lightly grease a baking sheet.

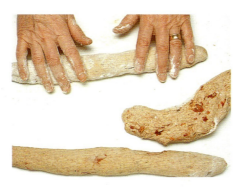

4 Turn the dough on to a lightly floured surface and knead for a few minutes. Divide the dough into 3 equal pieces and shape each into a sausage, about 33cm/13in long.

5 Join the three sausages on one end. Braid them together loosely, then press them together at the other end. Place on the baking sheet, cover and leave in a warm place for about 30 minutes until well risen. Preheat the oven to 220°C/425°F/Gas 7.

6 Sprinkle the braid with sea salt. Bake for 10 minutes, then lower the oven temperature to 200°C/400°F/Gas 6 and bake for a further 15–20 minutes or until the loaf sounds hollow when tapped.

INDEX